IP /895

6-
/a

BLOCK

Getting Out of Your Own Way

BLOCK

Getting Out of Your Own Way

The New Psychology of Counterintentional Behavior in Everyday Life

by Abigail Lipson Ph.D.
and
David N. Perkins, Ph.D.

A LYLE STUART BOOK
Published by Carol Publishing Group

A Lyle Stuart Book
Published By Carol Publishing Group

Editorial Offices
600 Madison Avenue
New York, NY 10022

Sales & Distribution Offices
120 Enterprise Avenue
Secaucus, NJ 07094

In Canada: Musson Book Company
A division of General Publishing Co. Limited
Don Mills, Ontario

Manufactured in the United States of America

Library of Congress Cataloging-in-Publication Data

Lipson, Abigail.
    Block--getting out of your own way : the new psychology of
    counterintentional behavior in everyday life / by Abigail Lipson
    and David N. Perkins.
        p.   cm.
    Includes bibliographical references.
    ISBN 0-8184-0516-3 : $18.95
        1. Intention. 2. Change (Psychology) 3. Failure (Psychology)
I. Perkins, David N. II. Title.
BF611.L56   1990
158'.9--dc20
                                                89-77879
                                                CIP

We dedicate this book
to our parents

The cases discussed in this book are amalgams
from a range of clinical and life experiences,
with no intended resemblance to any specific
individual.

CONTENTS

PART I

Building on Common Sense

How do we make sense of our own behavior, especially when we find ourselves ''blocked''—not behaving the way we meant to? When we're blocked, we often make sense of our dilemma by talking about ''psychological forces'' that overwhelm our intentions. Sometimes these explanations work pretty well. But sometimes they don't. We need more specific ideas about how psychological forces work to understand better why we get blocked.

PART II

Getting Blocked and Unblocked

When you're "blocked in," you can't stop doing something you want to stop doing. When you're "blocked out," you can't get going on something you want to do. Frequently, sheer will power doesn't solve the problem. But by depending less on sheer will power and more on using your will strategically, you can often outwit the "strong forces" causing your block.

We human beings mystify ourselves again and again with our own blocked behavior. "There's no good reason why I can't quit," you might say to yourself. Or "There's no good reason why I can't get started." But there's always a reason, though you may not *see* it at first. Often, *hidden* forces create blocks. To understand ourselves and avoid such blocks, we have to search out the hidden forces at work.

Insight certainly plays a role in "getting out of your own way," because you have to see just how you're *in* your own way to get out of it. But insight doesn't always automatically or magically solve problems of block. It helps in several specific ways we do well to keep in mind.

Have you ever been ashamed of your own anger, afraid of your own fear, or angry at your own weakness? When such things happen, you're experiencing ''second-order effects''—reactions to your own behavior and feelings. Such ''second-order effects'' often cause block. And knowing about them helps us to avoid the blocks they cause.

Remember the saying about potato chips: ''Nobody can eat just one.'' Many other patterns of behavior are like potato chips—once you start, it's hard to stop. We call these patterns of behavior ''thralls.'' By understanding why thralls grip us so strongly, we can avoid harmful thralls better. And get into *helpful* thralls more easily.

We all know someone—maybe ourselves—who seems to fall into the same kind of trap over and over again, for instance an unsatisfactory personal relationship. What causes these cycles and other complicated psychological binds, such as indecisiveness? Often, it's not a matter of one or two psychological forces at work, but a whole complicated "landscape" of forces. To find our way out of such difficulties, we need to see the "landscape" whole.

PART III

A Broader View

Let's review. To understand blocks and how to beat them, we have the idea of psychological forces plus five ways that blocks happen: strong forces, hidden forces, second-order forces, thrall, and many forces in an entrapping landscape.

All this talk about psychological forces is a theory. Like any theory, it deserves a critical look to size up its strengths and weaknesses. Moreover, the strengths and weaknesses for *you* will depend on how well you can use it to analyze your problems, and how at home you feel with its "poetry"—the metaphors and imagery it uses.

Acknowledgments

This book reflects several years of ongoing conversation, not only between the two of us but with many others. Our thanks go to all those who have had the patience and interest to explore with us the ideas in this book. Also, we want to acknowledge globally the many psychologists whose work has contributed to our thinking about block. While we believe that we have proposed a distinctive organization of ideas, few of these ideas begin with us.

Finally, we have several particular thanks to offer. We appreciate the vigorous editing of Kate Wilson during the preparation of the manuscript. We value Diane Downs for her logistical help in moving the manuscript toward publication. We are indebted to Dan Levy, our editor at Lyle Stuart, for his advice and support. And, finally, we thank the members of the Bureau of Study Counsel at Harvard University for their endless tolerance and good humor. And for all the coffee and cookies that we consumed in the preparation of this book.

Preface

ON THE USELESSNESS OF GOOD ADVICE

When we met in 1981—two psychologists with very different backgrounds and perspectives, arguing about the way the mind works—we discovered that, whatever our disagreements, we had a common question: Why do people do what they do? Especially, why do people do what they do, when it isn't what they *intend* to do?

For instance, you intend to stick to your exercise schedule. But rarely get to it. You intend to show up on time. But usually drag in late. You intend to cut down on smoking. But light up instead. You intend to make a will. But keep putting it off with flimsy excuses. You intend to make up with Betty or Ralph. But can't get yourself to make the first move.

What could be more normal? And what could be more strange! How is it that we human beings can intend to do one thing—and then find ourselves behaving in a completely different way, despite our best intentions? How is it that we're so often *blocked* from what we intend to do?

Well, we were fascinated by this question, so we went to work on it systematically. We pooled the perspectives of a clinical

15

psychologist concerned with people's inner experience and outward behavior, and a cognitive psychologist concerned with the way people process information. We kept on talking and arguing. We began to find some answers we pretty much agreed on. And we ended up with this book—the result of our different but equal contributions.

It won't take you long to discover that this book doesn't offer much in the way of flat-out advice. It's not that good advice is hard to give. On the contrary, it is cheap and easy to manufacture:

Are you troubled by procrastination? Do you constantly put off 'til tomorrow what you could do today? Well, here is a guaranteed cure for procrastination. Follow this advice and your procrastination problem will dissolve:

"Plan ahead. Start early."

Or are you concerned about your weight? Do you want to lose a few pounds? Well, here is a guaranteed weight loss method. Follow this advice and the pounds will melt away:

"Eat less. Exercise more."

These are examples of *good* advice. Guaranteed to work. All the same, we're confident that you recognize the uselessness of such advice. The moment you hear it, you know it doesn't speak to your real concerns. You *know* you should start earlier. You *know* you should eat less.

We try hard to keep such useless advice to a minimum in this book. Our effort, rather, is to explore with you why it often seems so hard to put even the best of advice into *effect*—why it is so hard to *get* yourself to follow your own good counsel. We hope to provide you with some ways of thinking about this puzzling issue which will help you become a better problem-solver with regard to your own intentions and behavior. We even end each chapter with a short list of what we call "ThinkAbouts"—not regimens to follow or how-to instructions, but interesting notions explored in the chapter that you might want to continue to ponder on your own.

So read on. We think you will find that we have written about some problems of the human condition that you share. And some strengths you have to cope with them.

A.L.
D.P.

BLOCK

Getting Out of Your Own Way

ON NOT DOING WHAT YOU THINK YOU SHOULD

For the good that I would, I do not: but evil which I would not, that I do.
—Romans 7:19

Jack says to Jill, "I have a new program of complete reform. It's up in the morning at 6:00 A.M. for a two mile jog. A brisk walk midday to freshen up. Then there's the 1,500 calorie per day diet, low cholesterol, low fat, high bulk. Also, I'm quitting smoking."

Jill says, "Wow! How long have you been on this plan?"

"I start tomorrow."

Both the comedy and the sly tragedy of this story come from our quick recognition that Jack probably will not start tomorrow, whatever his good intentions today. Instead, the morning will bring a postponement of the grand plan to the day after, or the week after, or the month after. Or, if Jack starts tomorrow, the plan will only survive a day or two. Simple living teaches us that we cannot so easily get ourselves to follow a strict regimen, despite the best of intentions.

21

Everyday life abounds with similar examples of actions falling short of intentions. Despite their best intentions, people routinely fail to mow the lawn, finish their income taxes, study the needed hours, prepare for a meeting, reconcile with a friend after an argument, and so on. Moreover, getting yourself *not* to do something is no easier—maybe even harder—than getting yourself to *do* something. People intend to quit drinking, nagging, staying up late, losing their tempers, and so on, but pretty frequently disappoint themselves. The failure of best intentions seems to be almost a badge of the human condition.

What Counterintentional Behavior Is and Isn't

Our name for this all-too-common shortfall is "*counterintentional behavior*": A person ends up behaving contrary to his or her own best intentions, although there is nothing that obviously prevents the person from following through on those intentions. For instance, Jack intends to start tomorrow and no physical barriers stand in the way, yet he does not. You mean to stop nagging your spouse or staying up late, but, despite your intentions, you find yourself nagging away or partying 'til dawn.

It's worth emphasizing that counterintentional behavior is not just any failure to follow through on intentions. Sometimes people fail to follow through because of external reasons. You want to visit Grandma for Thanksgiving, but the bridge is out, your car breaks down, or your three-year-old develops a fever of 103 degrees. Your failure to visit Grandma is not counterintentional behavior in our sense, even though it's behavior contrary to your intention. Also, sometimes people fail to follow through on intentions because of lack of ability. You mean to pass the exam, handle the job, win the race, and you apply yourself assiduously;

22

yet you just do not have the intelligence, expertise, or strength to pull it off. This also isn't counterintentional behavior in the sense we mean. Finally, sometimes intentions fall short not for lack of ability but for lack of good approach. You could have passed that test if only you had better skills for studying; you could have handled that job if only you knew better how to work with others; you could have won that race if only you had paced yourself more wisely. These situations too are not counterintentional behavior, although you did end up behaving in ways you didn't intend.

What's left? What is true counterintentional behavior? It's when you fail to do what your best judgment dictates, when nothing is really stopping you, not external barriers nor a lack of ability nor a lack of know-how. To put it another way, counterintentional behavior is a kind of failure of the will. You *could* do what you think you should, if only you could muster enough will power to carry through. Later we have a good deal to say about will power, arguing that it is actually a mistake to view counterintentional behavior as a lack of will power. But just as a way of picturing counterintentional behavior, one can think of it as behavior contrary to one's will, a problem that more will power would cure.

We said that when you behave counterintentionally, nothing really stands in the way of following your intentions. But "nothing" is a bit strong. To be sure, no external barriers or shortfalls of ability or know-how interfere. But something must stand in the way or you would behave intentionally.

That something we call *block*, and it gives our book its title. As if practical impediments to action and shortfalls of ability and know-how were not enough to trouble us, it seems that various psychological factors block us from doing what we think we should. But what are these psychological blocks? How do they

23

work? And what are the prospects of overcoming them? Studying these questions about block is the same as studying counterintentional behavior, because block and counterintentional behavior are simply two different ways of talking about the same thing.

Intentions, Best Intentions, and Real Intentions

But wait a minute. Do we really have counterintentional behavior in focus yet? Consider this paradoxical case. What if, rather than struggling ineffectually to behave as you intend, you readjust your intentions because you know yourself all too well. Let's say you want to quit smoking, you used to intend to quit smoking, you tried to quit several times, and now you have given up trying. You still think you should quit, you would like to quit, but you no longer *intend* to quit because you have readjusted your intentions to match more closely your behavior, rather than the other way around. Is your smoking still counterintentional behavior?

We say it is, because you're still blocked. Your behavior is counter to your "best" intentions. This is, if you thought you could successfully intend to quit smoking, you would. To put it another way without using the word intention, counterintentional behavior is behavior contrary to a person's best judgment about how he or she should behave.

There is a mischievous objection to this. One could argue that the whole idea of counterintentional behavior is empty because people always do what they "really" want to do! Jack may have intended yesterday to start his exercise regimen today, but today he no longer intends to start: He is doing exactly what he *really* wants, which is *not* to start. Likewise, if you've given up trying to quit smoking, you must really not want to quit: Indeed, you're doing exactly what you *really* intend, smoking away. Since people always do what they "really" intend to do, the notion of counterintentional behavior makes no sense.

At the core of this argument is an important point: People do end up behaving according to what you might call the "net effect" of the various motives in a situation. How could it be otherwise? Indeed, this notion of net effect of motives turns out to be very important as we look at block more deeply.

But, despite this kernel of insight, the notion that people always end up doing what they really intend won't hold water. Consider Jack again, and suppose he doesn't start the intended regimen. Jack follows "net motives," to be sure. But this does not mean that Jack feels good about it. On the contrary, he feels torn, divided, incapable. In fact, remember the emphasis on "best intentions." While Jack's net motives may dictate deferring the exercise and diet plan, his best intentions still say, "begin today," even as he is lounging on the couch with a strawberry sundae. In general, to say that people simply behave according to real intentions and let it go at that is to imply that they feel no tension, no strife, no division of self, no incongruence between best intentions and what actually occurs. This plainly is not the case.

The Importance of Counterintentional Behavior

Perhaps that's enough to define counterintentional behavior. But why does it deserve a book? Well, for one thing, there is certainly plenty of it! The several examples listed before are only the tip of a counterintentional iceberg. Counterintentional behavior is a routine part of life, a fundamental element of the human experience, a peculiarly unexalted part of what it is to be human.

Moreover, counterintentional behavior often does real harm.

People generally would be better off exercising more, smoking less, getting their studies done, and so on—and their families and friends would benefit too.

Besides the fact that counterintentional behavior usually runs contrary to your best interests, it hurts in itself. It's scary to see yourself divided in such a way. You have to wonder what control you can exercise over your fate. You have to doubt whether you are indeed the "captain of your soul." Existential ruminations aside, the tension between your best judgment and your actual behavior will make you very uncomfortable. When you break that diet, your guilt may turn your strawberry sundae sour.

Finally, although we're highlighting relatively commonplace blocks, they are by no means unserious for being commonplace. Everyday addictions to substances like cigarettes and alcohol become killers in many cases. Moreover, counterintentional behavior includes pathologies—drug addiction or bulimia, for instance. Indeed, we'll argue later on that the basic mechanisms of counterintentional behavior are not so very different in cases not ordinarily regarded as clinical problems and many cases calling for clinical intervention. To put it a little crudely, a lot of "crazy" behavior is not much different from "sane" behavior. People who act in crazy ways often can make decent judgments, and they often do not want to behave as they do. But they behave counterintentionally anyway—just like us "sane" folk. Unfortunately, their counterintentional behavior diverges intolerably from social conventions or is immediately harmful to themselves or to others. While focusing on more quotidian examples of counterintentional behavior, from time to time we'll touch on conventionally pathological examples and highlight the continuity between these and the everyday counterintentional behavior people take for granted.

Having introduced the theme and urged its importance, we should forecast what we plan to do about it. First, this book aims at understanding. In the pages that follow, we look at counterintentional behavior and the psychological blocks that create it— how they happen, why they happen, what underlying mechanisms are responsible. Counterintentional behavior turns out to be far more than one phenomenon. It can come about in a number of different ways that we review and relate to one another.

Besides understanding, there's the question of leverage. What can be *done* about blocks? A good deal, fortunately. Both everyday life and therapeutic practice are full of tactics that can moderate or dissolve blocks and reduce counterintentional behavior. People do not have to be as much the victims of themselves as they often are!

Part I

BUILDING ON COMMON SENSE

In order to make sense of our blocks, we must
start by looking at how we understand *any* of our
behavior. What common sense notions do we
use in our everyday thinking to explain why we
do what we do?

Chapter 1

COMMON SENSE
FOR COMMON BLOCKS

It's the morning of Andy's big presentation at his new job. As the sun starts to come up, he is asleep in his easy chair. A test pattern hums from the television set. Suddenly the national anthem blares, startling Andy awake. As his mind clears, the first thing he thinks is, "Oh, NO! How *could* I have spent all night in front of the TV? I *knew* I had to prepare for my presentation today!"

We have all asked ourselves such questions. "Why did I lose my temper? I knew I would regret it." "Why did I take that first drink? I knew where it would lead." "How could I have eaten that second piece of pie? I knew I'd get a stomach ache." The familiar sound of these voices testifies to our capacity to behave in ways contrary to our best intentions, even when "we know better." We can mystify ourselves by our very own behavior.

Counterintentional behavior—behaving contrary to your own best intentions. What a nuisance! Sometimes, what a disaster! And what a puzzle! If there's one thing to be said for counterintentional behavior, at least it makes us think. Usually, we don't bother thinking about why we do what we do. We just *do*, and

31

it's done, and we go *do* something else. But when counter-intentional behavior arises—then we feel truly confounded: *Why would we do things that are not at all what our best intentions recommend?*

Happily, our counterintentional behavior doesn't usually pre-occupy us for long. For one thing, we seem to know ourselves too well to be shocked by many of our little everyday lapses: you mean to return that phone call but you keep forgetting; you intend to keep an eye on that pie in the oven but you get distracted. Par for the course. We don't expect ourselves to behave perfectly and intentionally every moment of our lives. Something in us may even say, "Of course not; that wouldn't be human!"

For another thing, we don't stay preoccupied with our counter-intentional behavior for long because it makes a certain amount of sense to us. Yes, without any technical psychological language or psychotherapist on call, we can and do explain to ourselves much of our counterintentional as well as intentional behavior.

Indeed, people have a solid sensible theory of why they do or don't behave as they mean to behave. Of course, this theory is not written down in books. It's *implicit* in our assumptions, *tacit* in the way we talk, *latent* in the ways we handle situations. But it's there. And it's a pretty good theory.

The purpose of this chapter is to articulate the common-sense theory that underlies the way people make sense of their everyday behavior. Not only because it's a pretty good theory, but also because it's a point of departure. Once articulated, this common-sense theory supplies a mother lode of ideas that can be extended to help us understand more puzzling blocks. Later chapters of this book examine such extensions and elaborations of the everyday theory. But we dedicate this first chapter to the basics—to the genius of our common sense.

Force: The Latent Metaphor

The essence of metaphor is understanding and experiencing one kind of thing in terms of another.

—Lakoff & Johnson

What is this shy theory that proves so useful without ever announcing itself as such? One way to scare it out of its burrow is to look at our language when we talk about why we do what we do. All of us say things like this:

"I felt drawn to him." "It was just force of habit." "They pushed me into it." "All it took was will power." "I didn't have the energy." "I couldn't get moving." "I felt compelled to." In speaking of our goals, we say that something is "attractive," "engaging," "compelling," "hard," "resistant" or "repellent."

Phrases like these use fairly blatantly what might be called a "force metaphor." We speak of motives, causes and reasons in our psychological world the way we speak of forces in the physical world. Listen to some of this "force talk" again and notice how rich and dynamic an account of behavior it gives: We feel *drawn* to things or *pulled* into them. Things *resist* us or *push* us around. Habits have force—in fact we name it *force of habit*. We talk about the will as a force we can wield to good effect if we have enough will *power*. We talk about *being on a roll* and describe our behavior as having *momentum* or *inertia*. We talk about objects in our world exerting forces of *attraction* or *repulsion* with regard to our behavior. The very word *motive* has a force connotation; a motive is whatever *moves* us to action. And a *block*, of course, is something that stands in the way of our efforts to behave as we intend.

33

To spell out the metaphor a little, we talk as though we get pushed around—or push ourselves around, in the case of will power—in a space of possible behaviors. How we behave depends on the net result of the forces at work, just as the movement of an object in a physical space is the net result of the forces operating on it.

Of course, not all our ways of explaining our actions involve such explicit force talk. Many terms—emotional or physiological terms, for example—make no direct allusion to the force metaphor. When people speak words like "hunger," "thirst," "lust," "fear," "anger," "love" or "sadness," the metaphor of common-sense physics fades into the background. But a careful look shows that it is not so far in the background as it might at first appear. We freely mix force terms with other sorts of words as though they were kin, saying, for instance, "I think I've *fallen* in *love*," or "I was *thirsty* for a beer and I just couldn't *resist*," or "I feel so *sad* and *depressed* today." We even speak of being *driven* by fear or anger. In other words, although terms such as hunger, thirst, fear and sadness do not on the face of it refer to forces, some of the ways we *use* these terms suggests that we consider hunger, thirst, etc., themselves to be forces of particular sorts—the hunger force, the thirst force, and so on.

This is not to say that the force metaphoric system is the *only* metaphoric system good for making common sense of everyday behavior, counterintentional and otherwise. Other metaphors, other concepts play important roles too. Our last chapter explores this issue, discussing some of the limits of the force metaphor and placing it in a larger context. But for now, let's simply recognize the force metaphor as just that, a powerful metaphor, and a useful sense-making tool.

Everyday Force Theory

We strive in spite of ourselves, as a natural expression of our integrity, to make sense of our experiences, our feelings, and our knowledge.

—Kiyo Morimoto

Here we have Andy in agony over messing up his big presentation for his new job. And other people in agony over their own episodes of counterintentional behavior. And lots more people who are just annoyed. And we say that people have a tacit theory that helps them to make sense of their own everyday behavior, including counterintentional behavior. And we say it's a pretty good theory, "the genius of our common sense."

Yet all we've talked about so far is a metaphor. Psychological "forces." Just a metaphor!

It is remarkable that within this mere metaphor there actually *is* a theory with explanatory power. We'll give it a name, Everyday Force Theory. And we'll take a closer look at it, to see just what sort of a theory it is.

One way to examine a theory is to treat it formally, spelling out its basic principles or axioms. In the case of Everyday Force Theory, the axioms are implicit in the way people talk about and think about why they do what they do. But the axioms are very much *there*, shaping our thinking about the whys and wherefores of our lives. Let's try to spell out the implicit axioms that make up Everyday Force Theory. Then we can see how, quite automatically as we think and talk, they help us to make sense of why we do what we do—including counterintentional behavior.

1. We infer psychological forces from their effects.
   In physics, you don't *see* forces in the same straightforward

35

way that you see a lever or an inclined plane. You infer the presence of forces to explain why things happen. For example, scientists infer the existence of the force of gravity from observations of falling objects. It's the same for psychological forces: People infer the presence of psychological forces from their observations of human behavior. For instance, we don't *see* the psychological forces that kept Andy watching TV and then sleeping away the night in front of it. We simply *infer* what the forces might have been: a gripping thriller on the tube, fear of facing his boss, or whatever. In physics and psychology alike, a force is not something we perceive directly, but a way we have of explaining the events we *do* perceive directly.

This notion raises some interesting questions: Can *anything* then qualify as a psychological force: an emotion, an idea, a neurochemical state, an intention? Are forces even *real* or just labels? We will return to these questions later on.

2. Psychological forces (like force vectors in physics) have direction and magnitude.

When we say that hunger motivates our behavior, we can ask, "Hunger for *what*? Steak or tofu?" Our hunger is directing us *towards* something. Even if we feel just plain *hungry*, it's a good bet we're hungry for food rather than for ballpoints or Brillo. It also makes sense to ask, "*How* hungry?" Forces can be strong or weak or anything in between. In general, people think of psychological forces in ways that involve direction and magnitude.

3. Psychological forces combine to yield a net effect.

Force of habit, your hunger for popcorn, and a good review of a film may all conspire to urge you to go to the movies this Friday night, different though the contributing forces are from one another. Indeed, note how *very* diverse they are. A force of habit is usually not felt as a desire so much as an impulse. The popcorn may be felt as a rich and active craving. And the good review may

36

engage your intellectual interest. Yet this patchwork of very different motives yields a combined net effect, and off you go.

4. Psychological forces in the same direction reinforce one another and psychological forces in contrary directions inhibit one another.

If force of habit *and* a yen for popcorn encourage you to attend the Friday movie, you will feel driven to go at least a little more than if only one of these forces were operating alone. If force of habit encourages you to go, but at the same time your plan for a long excursion on Saturday tells you to stay at home and get some sleep, you will feel less moved to go.

However, note that forces in the same direction don't necessarily *strictly* sum their power. For instance, suppose that force of habit alone makes the Friday movie attractive and popcorn hunger alone makes the movie equally attractive. This doesn't mean that both together will make the movie exactly twice as attractive. Just more attractive than either alone. Likewise, opposite forces inhibit one another, but they don't necessarily strictly subtract. We might say that psychological forces obey not a *strict* but a *weak* additivity rule: forces add to and subtract from one another, but not in a precise mathematical way.

Spelled out so formally, these axioms make Everyday Force Theory sound quite impressive. Of course, Everyday Force Theory is not nearly as *precise* as a physicist's theory of physical forces, with its exact mathematical predictions. But perhaps we shouldn't expect Everyday Force Theory to be very precise: human motivations are simply not as neat as physical forces. Everyday Force Theory is about as exact as human behavior allows.

Are Psychological Forces Real?

Everyday Force Theory *sounds* like a pretty good theory. But surely there is something deceptive about all this. After all, speaking of psychological forces is just a metaphor. Psychological forces aren't real.

Or are they? We human beings have made up such notions as gravity to explain phenomena we observe. And gravity is "real." Psychological forces, no more or less than physical forces, are real in that both are cognitive constructions designed by human beings in an effort to make sense of the world.

Look at it this way: We *create* reality by symbolizing it—reality only exists for us as whatever we construe reality to be. If we can define a notion of psychological forces, apply it consistently across a diversity of situations, and confirm that these supposed forces seem to obey the rules we expect them to, this *makes* forces real. That is all there *is* to being real. Things we consider unimpeachably real, such as stones and sneezes, meet no stronger criteria than these.

There's one more comment worth making about the reality of psychological forces. Quite apart from such philosophical justifications, psychological forces *feel* like forces. We feel *drawn* to the extra slice of strawberry pie in the cupboard, *repelled* by the accumulation of junk in the basement, led along *forcibly* by a bad habit. This is often true in a palpable physical sense. You may find your hand dipping into the bag for another potato chip almost as though someone else were manipulating it. Is that really *your* hand, you wonder? If you try to resist, the hand ignores you completely, or even seems to fight back against the power of your will. Your mind flashes to scenes from the movie *Dr. Strangelove* in which Peter Sellers has to wrestle with his own hand to keep it from killing him! Anyway, the point is that psychological forces are as real as our very real feelings and experiences.

How Everyday Force Theory
Explains Counterintentional Behavior
and Other Human Problems

Counterintentional behavior often leaves us feeling torn. When our actual behavior differs from our intended behavior, we become acutely aware of the disparity. At times, it's merely annoying, as when you realize you have managed to put off writing a thank-you note for yet another day. At times, it's extremely painful, as when you find yourself going for the cookies despite the diet you swore you would stick to. The rift between our intention and our behavior not only puzzles us but disturbs us.

When such things happen, the question we ask ourselves is not simply a puzzled "Why did I do that?" but a pained "WHY did I *DO* that?" What we are asking ourselves is probably, "How could I have been so *helpless*," "How could I have been so *weak*," or "How could I have been so *stupid*?" Everyday Force Theory offers us several ways of understanding our moments of counterintentional helplessness, weakness or stupidity.

"How Could I Have Been So Helpless?"

Looking back on our actions, we sometimes feel as though we were suddenly "carried away" by forces which led us to behave counterintentionally. We are appalled at how quickly and easily our intentions were overruled. We shake our heads and think, "I didn't have a chance . . . How could I have been so helpless?"

Our everyday force talk offers an explanation. Often we interpret counterintentional behavior as the result of an overwhelming combination of forces. Take, for example, a situation in which your best intentions are to lose weight and yet you find yourself eating a chocolate sundae. If forces at work can be inferred from behavior, and you are counterintentionally eating a chocolate sundae, then according to Everyday Force Theory there must be a pretty powerful chocolate-sundae-eating force at work. Your intentions may act as a sundae-*shunning* force, but if you are, in fact, eating the sundae, then your intentions must have been overcome by a sundae-*eating* force of greater magnitude. This is the "brute force" explanation of counterintentional behavior: The stronger force always wins out.

Sometimes a brute force explanation fails to satisfy us; it doesn't ring true. What if the sundae you are eating is pistachio, which isn't your favorite flavor but which you ordered because they were all out of chocolate. In this case, not only do you want to lose weight very badly, but at the same time you're not finding great joy in the sundae. It doesn't *feel* like there are very powerful sundae-eating forces at work—certainly not sundae-eating forces strong enough to outweigh your strong desire to lose weight. Yet here you are, eating the sundae anyway.

We often explain situations like this to ourselves by a slightly more complex version of the brute force theory, which suggests that it may not be the strongest force that wins out, but the strongest combination of forces. The so-so taste of the sundae alone may not amount to much of a force in comparison to your strong motivation to lose weight. However, our everyday force talk suggests that diverse forces can pool their effects according to the "weak additivity" rule. Liking the taste of the sundae, *and* feeling the heat of the day, *and* being tired of walking around, *and* having some time to kill before your bus arrives, *and* feeling like you deserve a treat for having had such a rotten day all may combine forces to overwhelm your strong intention to stick to your diet.

Notice that the brute force explanation can leave us feeling even more helpless than we already feel. After all, there is nothing one can do in the face of overwhelming forces. We can rant and rave and reaffirm our intentions, even as we behave counterintentionally, but according to Everyday Force Theory, we are powerless to behave in any other way.

In this sense, brute force explanations have a deterministic quality that we greet with mixed feelings. On the one hand, we may feel depressed or angry when a brute force explanation robs us of our sense of free will. On the other hand, we may feel some relief from guilt when a brute force explanation comfirms our sense that our counterintentional behavior is "not our fault." Overall, people find brute force explanations quite serviceable and rely upon them fairly often as a way of understanding counterintentional behavior.

"How Could I Have Been So Weak?"

We are often especially dismayed with ourselves when we realize that we have behaved counterintentionally while all the while exerting *active effort* to behave intentionally. That is, we *willed* ourselves to behave according to our best intentions and yet "for reasons beyond our control," we found ourselves behaving in another way. Afterwards, we shake our heads and think, "I tried and I tried. . . . How could I have been so weak?"

In our everyday force talk, we often understand counterintentional behavior as a failure of the will. We expect a lot of the will: We like to believe that the will is a strong force that we can match up against opposing forces with pretty good odds of victory. In situations of counterintentional behavior, therefore, Everyday Force Theory suggests that the will has experienced some sort of power failure.

According to everyday force talk, failures of will power occur in two ways. First, it's widely believed that people differ in terms of "how much" will power they've got. We hear people say "I have *no* will power," or "He's got *lots* of will power." Will power determines the magnitude of counterintentional forces a person can withstand before actually behaving counterintentionally. Thus, faced with identical situations, one individual may behave intentionally while another behaves counterintentionally; the former has "more" will power than the latter.

The second way Everyday Force Theory accounts for failure of the will concerns fluctuations within the individual. We all have our weak moments now and then, our good days and bad days. We might suffer a failure of the will the way we suffer a brief cold. In addition, the power of the individual will might fluctuate as particular temptations afflict a generally strong constitution. For example, you may have a will of iron that nevertheless melts in the presence of your only weakness, Godiva chocolate-covered cherries.

Our force talk, then, assumes that will power is a fairly strong force, although it differs in magnitude from person to person and lapses occasionally even in the strongest-willed individuals. Counterintentional behavior gets blamed either on an individual's inherent lack of will power or on a lapse or glitch in the normally robust will. Notice that Everyday Force Theory also assumes the importance of the will in pro-intentional behavior: whereas counterintentional behavior signals a failure of will, pro-intentional behavior signals a success. Later in the book we'll take a sharp look at how sound these ideas are.

"How Could I Have Been So Stupid?"

Looking back on our own counterintentional behavior, we sometimes feel amazed and ashamed that we did what we did. We can't exactly say we were overcome by more powerful forces, as a brute force explanation might suggest, and we can't exactly say that we tried our best only to be let down by the weakness of our will. Rather, we feel as though we allowed ourselves to be bamboozled into behaving counterintentionally despite our better judgment. We look back and think, "I should've known better . . . How could I have been so stupid?"

In other words, in some situations, our judgment in the moment of acting gets warped by strong forces. We only realize in retrospect—too late—that, had we stopped to think, we would have behaved quite differently. We would have made a wiser judgment and marshalled the power of our will to act on it. Instead, we came under the influence of strong forces that clouded our judgment.

Say for example you are in a hurry to pack for a trip, but you just have time to put through a quick load of laundry before you go. You throw your new red sweater in with everything else: it occurs to you that the sweater is liable to run, which would be a disaster, but you are in a rush so you go ahead and toss it in. Only when you discover that all your whites have turned to pinks, do

you realize that your judgment at the moment was clouded: you certainly didn't *intend* to ruin all your clothes. Your actions were influenced by being in hurry, by wanting to take that sweater with you, by not wanting to pack dirty clothes, etc. In retrospect, you realize how stupid you were. If you had stopped to ask yourself, "Would I rather leave this sweater behind or have all my laundry turn pink?" you would have chosen to leave the sweater behind. Your regrets afterwards arise not because you have "learned your lesson" from the experience; you *knew* the lesson beforehand. You knew that new dark clothes often run when they are first washed, and you knew that you were throwing your red sweater in with your light laundry. Everyday Force Theory would say in situations like this that strong forces clouded your judgment.

In summary, our everyday force talk provides us with several very useful ways of understanding our own and others' instances of counterintentional behavior. We might behave counterintentionally when we are overcome by strong forces, when we experience a failure of the will, or when our judgment gets clouded.

Although these explanations are quite serviceable in many everyday situations, looked at a little more closely they have some serious limitations that can mislead us and mystify us in situations like this that strong forces clouded your judgment.

efforts to understand our more paradoxical cases of counterintentional behavior. Some of the limits of Everyday Force Theory are described at the end of this chapter.

Additional Ways in Which We Use Everyday Force Theory

Besides helping to explain counterintentional behavior, we use Everyday Force Theory to make sense of other aspects of human behavior. Among these are: how individuals differ from one another; how we define "normal" human behavior, and what causes psychological stress.

Individual Differences

People react to the world in very different—sometimes unpredictably different—ways. For example, I may like vanilla while you like chocolate. I may like Janis Joplin a lot while you don't like her at all. Our everyday force talk acknowledges that the same factor or stimulus may call into play very different forces for different people.

Remember, forces are like vectors: they have direction and magnitude. Sometimes, people differ in the *direction* of the forces at work. For example, *you* may be absolutely fascinated by airplanes: you built models as a kid, you are a Frequent Flier, and you subscribe to *Pilot* magazine. At the same time, *I* may be terrified of airplanes: I hate heights, I always go Greyhound, and my palms sweat at the very thought of boarding a plane. Airplanes bring out in you a force of similar magnitude (strong) but different direction (towards vs. away from) than the force they bring out in me. I am as repulsed by airplanes as you are attracted to them.

Sometimes, people differ in the magnitude of the forces at work. For example, you and I may both like going to the movies, but I may like it a lot more than you do; or you and I may both dislike going to the dentist, but you may dislike it a lot more than I do. Movies and dentists engender in you and me forces of similar direction but different magnitude.

In our everyday understandings of the world, we not only accept these individual differences in force-reactions, we expect them. For example, when we want to get to know people we may ask them who their favorite author is or what sort of activities they enjoy. Similarly, when we want to give someone a special birthday present, we may think long and hard to come up with something that will engender in them particularly strong positive forces. Everyday Force Theory allows for these broad variations in force magnitude and direction from one individual to the next.

Normalcy

But even the considerable latitude that Everyday Force Theory allows has its limits. In our everyday theorizing about the world, we can't entirely avoid thinking of things as being attractive or repulsive *in their own rights*. We often think of things as being "good" or "bad" or "scary" or "pleasing" or whatever, not just in the eye of the beholder, but in and of themselves. For example, we think of a hot stove as dangerous: We know it might burn us, so of course we are repulsed at the thought of putting our hand down on the hot grill. The danger is "really" in the stove, and the avoidance forces that the hot stove engenders in us are a function of this reality, not merely of personal preference.

The notion that things have a "proper" or "appropriate" degree of force associated with them helps us define what is "normal" behavior. For example, we all know that being bothered by a mosquito is unpleasant, but being attacked by a mad dog is *extremely* unpleasant. This certainly allows us to establish some norms of expectable and acceptable behavior. If by some chance, you see someone run away screaming from an encounter with a mosquito, you think, "something must be *wrong* with her."

Most often, violations of commonly held understandings about what's good or bad, what's to be sought and what's to be shunned, make us suspect sickness or mistakenness. For example, if someone shows no regard for the danger of the hot stove, we are likely to think they are either crazy (perhaps self-destructive) or somehow misinformed (as with a small child who hasn't yet learned that stoves are hot, or an adult who doesn't know that the stove is on).

We demand these standards of normalcy not only from other people, but from ourselves as well. If we find *ourselves* behaving in ways that we think are excessive or inadequate or inappropriate given the degree and direction of the forces we "know" are appropriate, we feel that something is amiss and we question our motivations.

Stress

Counterintentional behavior often brings with it an experience of inner tension or stress. But stress also often occurs when we behave according to our best intentions. So what is tension or stress? According to Everyday Force Theory, we think of psychological forces causing tension in the same way that physical forces produce tension: stress results when a force meets a counterforce, when a force meets a barrier, or when forces are working at cross-purposes.

The language we use to talk about inner tension is rich with force talk. The words "stress" and "tension," for example, are borrowed from the vocabulary we use to describe conditions in the physical world. We describe ourselves as being "stuck," "in a bind" or "all bottled up," when some force within or without us gets held back from expression. When we feel ourselves being drawn in different directions by the operation of incompatible forces we say we are "torn apart" or we are "barely holding it together." If we are "under tremendous pressure," we may feel we are approaching a "breaking point" or that we are "about to crack."

Everyday Force Theory takes it as a given that forces in conflict (or forces otherwise prevented from expression) produce stress. We rely on this assumption to help us understand ourselves and others in an important way. When we experience forces in opposition in a situation, then we by definition experience stress. If we encounter stress, then by definition the situation involves opposed forces. These assumptions are the case whether we ultimately behave intentionally or counterintentionally. We may not be aware of the stress in the first instance and we may not be aware of the stressors in the second instance, but Everyday Force Theory tell us that they are there nonetheless.

Some Limits of Everyday Force Theory

Let's summarize what we've said so far about Everyday Force Theory. Force talk has a job to do—making sense out of how we behave and why. Whether we behave as we expect to or whether we surprise ourselves, the tacit theory underlying force talk helps us to understand ourselves. Indeed, Everyday Force Theory does pretty well as a first-cut theory of human behavior and human foibles. First of all, it offers a straightforward account of why people do what they do in everyday life. Marsha goes to work on Monday for the pay, cameraderie, involvement in her work, prestige, and similar factors not outweighed by onerous duties, the lure of South Sea islands, intermittent boredom, and so on. In general, we behave according to the net effect of various forces of various types.

When we conduct ourselves contrary to our best intentions, our force talk helps us again to understand what's going on. Counter-intentional behavior occurs when forces conspire to sweep us along ("How could I be so helpless?"), overwhelm our wills ("How could I be so weak?"), or cloud our judgment ("How could I be so stupid?"). Moreover, stress and individual differences in motives also lend themselves to explanation through force talk: conflicting forces yield stress and differences in motivation from person to person reflect magnitudes of force specific to the person.

With all that said, however, our tacit Everyday Force Theory does not do the perfect and seamless job of accounting for our conduct that it might. We human beings have a penchant for paradox, it seems, and we frequently manage to puzzle and dismay ourselves with blocks and other dilemmas that pass beyond the reach of everyday force talk. The chapters that follow examine some human foibles not so readily accommodated by Everyday Force Theory and explore how an extended theory might deal with them. Let's preview some of the assumptions within Everyday Force Theory that need to be questioned.

The will is usually strong—or is it? Everyday Force Theory treats the will as a strong force subject to exceptions: some people have weak wills and most of us occasionally prove weak-willed. However, perhaps the will is not so generally strong as we like to think. Most situations do not really test its strength, because in most situations our best intentions accord with the trend of other forces anyway; our wills simply add to the trend. For instance, many forces recommend that Marsha drag out of bed, grab a hasty breakfast, and run for the bus. Her actual application of will power is only one part of the picture. And what happens when strong forces run counter to our best intentions? Then it seems that all too often our will to pursue our best intentions does little good. In Chapter 2, we look at the problem of overwhelming forces with more care and reassess the role of the will in overcoming counterintentional behavior and fostering self-control.

Forces are mostly overt—or are they? Our force talk treats forces by and large as overt entities, as though we need only glance at ourselves and our circumstances to feel them at work and identify them. However, a major tenet of many psychological theories is that the forces producing our behavior are often not so obvious. People commonly do things without knowing why and without being able to discover why. Forces that a person refuses to acknowledge influence behavior even as their existence is denied. A force that was originally directed against one person in particular—say resentfulness towards an overdominant father—may become displaced and play itself out in unrecognized form against other persons or things—say in a silly argument with the boss. In Chapter 3, we explore the nature of such "hidden" forces.

Counterintentional behavior is cured by insight—or is it? As a rule, we are highly motivated to understand our own behavior. Indeed, Everyday Force Theory has evolved as a result of this very desire for insight. In general, we expect that insight into the forces at work producing our behavior will help us to control our behavior. Despite this expectation, though, we all know that insight doesn't automatically or magically solve our counterintentional problems, although we might wish it would. In Chapter 4, we explore the role of insight in our efforts to cope with counterintentional behavior, and specify why and when insight does help.

We react primarily to the forces in the external world—or do we? Our force talk mostly addresses forces as though they come from opportunities and threats outside ourselves; we want to achieve this gain, avoid that loss, and so on. But in corners of our everyday speech, we find evidence to indicate that matters are not so simple. For instance, people speak of "fear of fear itself," or of being ashamed of their fear. In general, people have strong reactions not only to events in the world but to their own actual or potential feelings about those events. These reactions reflect what we will call *second-order forces*. Many emotions that trouble people implicate second-order forces at least as much as first-order forces. For instance, when someone feels blocked in trying to achieve something difficult, fear of the shame of failure may figure just as much as the actual consequences of failure, such as losing one's job. Everyday Force Theory does not exclude second-order forces, but makes no special place for them. In Chapter 5, we do.

Forces are pretty constant—or are they? It is easiest to think of forces as acting constantly on a particular person, who behaves according to one force and then another. Plainly, though, forces vary according to environmental stimuli and physiological state. If you encounter a cream puff, you are likely to find yourself in the grip of a cream-puff-eating-force that would never have arisen without the stimulus of the visible cream puff, and all the more so if you are hungry. But, beyond this obvious point, forces can vary drastically depending on what you are doing moment to moment. While engrossed in a good mystery novel, you may find that other activities and even duties draw you very little—the lawn work or your math assignment can wait. If distracted by a phone call, however, you may discover that the spell has been broken, and you'll turn to something else. In general, how much an activity enthralls you varies depending on whether you are already involved in the activity or not. This phenomenon, which we call *thrall*, helps to explain drinking and eating binges as well as a number of other compulsive human behaviors, some benign and some even productive. Chapter 6 gives particular attention to thrall and related matters.

Vacillation is indecision—or is it? Another oddity of human behavior occurs when we find ourselves caught between two or more options. A and B are both attractive, but you can't make up your mind and so do nothing and get the advantages of neither.

Or A and B are both undesirable, and, unable to commit yourself to the lesser of the evils, you find yourself falling willy-nilly into one or the other as circumstances unfold. Usually we think about vacillation as a cognitive failure of decision making processes; we say that we cannot make up our minds. Such circumstances, however, often are better understood in terms of forces and the way forces change as we think of going with option A or going with option B. Chapter 7 looks at indecision with the thought that it often reflects a play of forces rather than a cognitive lapse.

Reality is really real—or is it? Our force talk assumes a backdrop of reality where the world behaves in a certain way and various forces have "proper" weights. You may overreact or underreact to the threat of a bee sting: but a bee sting is a bee sting, a bee sting hurts just so much, and that "real" degree of hurt defines the proper magnitude of a "bee avoiding force." Someone extremely undermotivated to avoid bees (who goes looking for bee nests to stomp on) or someone extremely over-motivated to avoid bees (who jumps up and runs away screaming if you say "buzz") appears crazy or childish or otherwise not "normal." This objectivist posture, of course, neglects the point that force norms and even the notion of force itself are human constructions. People of different cultures, personal histories and characters may find Everyday Force Theory—and the more so-phisticated version developed in the remainder of this book— more or less useful. Taking a step back from any theory and evaluating it as a theory in a larger context can be a helpful exercise in assessing the theory's usefulness. We first summarize Force Theory and then take this step back from it in Chapters 8 and 9.

These paragraphs make plain how all is not well in the land of

Everyday Force Theory. When theories give trouble, one natural move is to demolish them and rebuild from the ground up. In this spirit, we could dismiss force talk as naïve and limiting, forget about the underlying Everyday Force Theory, and seek different foundations upon which to build a model of human motivation. However, we believe that Everyday Force Theory offers an important core of common sense and sound principles, and we can imagine ways in which we might productively explore and expand upon them. So, as the following chapters unfold, we adopt Everyday Force Theory as the core of an explicit theory, augment it, and see what sense an extended Force Theory can make of the paradoxes of human conduct.

ThinkAbouts

What does all this mean to you? *How might you continue
to think about the ideas presented in this chapter?*

• Practice becoming more aware of your counterintentional
behavior—not just your big blocks, but little everyday ones as
well. Reflecting on how you routinely manage little blocks can
help you to figure out how to manage big blocks.

• Try to pay attention to the "force talk" you use in your
everyday speech—your metaphors of force, energy, movement,
power, etc. Your "force talk" reflects some underlying assumptions about human behavior that you can't readily examine until
you make them explicit.

• When you notice yourself thinking, "How could I have been
so *helpless*?"—think some more! Ask yourself, "*How* could I
have been so helpless? What forces were carrying me away?"

• When you notice yourself thinking, "How could I have been so
weak?"—think some more! You may be expecting too much
from your will power. Ask, "*How* could I have been so weak?
What strong forces were working on me?"

• When you notice yourself thinking, "How could I have been so
stupid?"—think some more! Practice catching yourself in mid-

act when you suspect that you are behaving mindlessly. Ask, "*How* could I have been so stupid? What forces were clouding my better judgment?"

• Try to be alert to those times when everyday ways of making sense of your own behavior seem to fail you—ways in which Everyday Force Theory is misleading or incomplete. Here is where a more extended force theory may help you toward a better understanding of why you behave as you do.

Part II

GETTING BLOCKED
AND UNBLOCKED

Common sense can't always help us understand our behavior when we're blocked—behaving contrary to our best intentions. We need to look beyond common sense to develop new ways of thinking about the causes and cures of block.

Chapter 2

BLOCKED IN, BLOCKED OUT

The Role of Strong Forces

When very bright people do very stupid things, we know we are in the presence of powerful forces.
—William G. Perry, Jr.

Reginald lies fast asleep. Suddenly, his alarm clock rings. Startled awake, he reaches over to turn off the buzzer. As his head slumps back to the pillow, he thinks, "What's today? Tuesday. I have a meeting at 9:00. I've got to get up." He lies under the covers, inert, awake, thinking, "I've got to get up . . . I'll wear my gray suit . . . Get up . . . " But he can't seem to get going. When Reginald finally swings his legs out of bed, he glances at the clock and realizes that he's going to be late. "What a jerk I am," he thinks, rushing to dress. "I can't believe I've just been lying here, wide awake, letting the time slip by. I'm such a wimp for not getting up with the damn alarm."

Hermione's deadline is only days away. Like any professional writer, she sometimes gets assignments that seem to be more trouble than they're worth. This is one of them. Finishing her coffee, Hermione contemplates moving over to her desk. But then she notices the dirty dishes piled up in the sink. "Better neaten the place up a bit before I settle down to write," she says. One thing leads to another, and it isn't until late that night, as she is drifting off to sleep, that Hermione realizes another day has gone by and she hasn't written a word. Hermione feels frustrated and angry with herself. "If I tried harder I could have started this thing a lot earlier and stuck to a schedule. All it takes is a little will power, a little discipline," she thinks. "Tomorrow," she promises herself, "tomorrow I'll get to work right after breakfast."

Reginald and Hermione deserve a sympathetic smile—or an empathetic groan. Their experiences are all-too-recognizable examples of everyday counterintentional behavior. Reginald feels trapped in an activity he wants to escape: lying in bed. Hermione feels repelled by a task she intends to do: writing at her desk.

"Blocked in" and "blocked out" are handy names for the two basic force situations behind experiences like those of Reginald and Hermione. "Blocked in" describes a pattern of forces that leaves you unable, despite your best efforts, to *disengage* from some behavior you *don't* want. "Blocked out" describes forces that leave you unable, despite your best efforts, to *engage* in some behavior that you *do* want.

"Blocked in" and "blocked out" share a painfully familiar pattern. You begin with clear and good intentions. Then—whoops—you find you have behaved counterintentionally. So you decide that you need "a little more will power." Surely some self-discipline is all that's called for! You're confident, furthermore, that the discipline you need lies somewhere within most people, including yourself. You resolve to "try harder."

Despite your resolutions, however, the will fails to overcome the opposing forces at work. Once again, you catch yourself staying in bed, avoiding dismal tasks, overeating, overspending, or whatever. You end up feeling like a jerk: guilty, weak-willed and frustrated.

Of course, the pattern is familiar, but that makes it no less puzzling, and certainly no less frustrating. How is it that we *get* blocked? What is it that *keeps* us blocked? And, most painfully, why are our willful efforts to unblock ourselves so *ineffective*?

The Myth of Will Power

Our common sense understanding of "blocked in" and "blocked out"—that is, what Everyday Force Theory says— includes an important assumption: The will is a strong force. We can pit it against most other forces with some success; the stronger the offending force, the more will power we need to apply.

How does this key assumption shape our understanding of everyday counterintentional behavior? For one thing, our belief in a strong will often leads us, just like Reginald in the opening scenario, to blame counterintentional behavior on a weakness or failure of will. After all, we figure, when the will is operating full throttle, we should have no trouble acting according to our best judgement. So counterintentional behavior means there's an episodic (or worse, permanent) failure of the normally strong will. Or, like Hermione, we blame our counterintentional behavior on insufficient effort. We figure all we need is a blast of the will at a higher volume. So we resolve to "try harder next time."

Why do we believe in a strong will? Such beliefs help us to make an effort to cope. We tell ourselves, "If at first you don't succeed—try, try again." We pep talk ourselves into achieving difficult goals that we might not otherwise manage.

But our belief in the strength of our will power doesn't quite make sense. If the will is normally so strong, why is counterintentional behavior so common? And why does it so maddeningly resist the "try harder" strategy? Everyday experience gives us ample reason to feel skeptical about the supposed strength of our wills.

Let's consider the possibility that the will is not usually so strong after all. Indeed, the will is rather a weak force, as forces go. When we behave intentionally, it is not because our will is especially strong and when we behave counterintentionally, it is not because our will is especially weak. Rather, in both situations, forces other than—and stronger than—our will direct us.

Suppose we consider the will a weak player, rather than a strong one. How would we have to understand situations differently? First, consider a situation where behavior matches intentions: Bartholemew sticks to his exercise schedule. Now, if the will is not so very strong, he can't be doing this by force of will alone. So we have to wonder about the other factors contributing to his success. With a little thought, it's not hard to identify some of them. He enjoys the company of his racquetball partner; he hates the way he looks and feels when he's out of shape; he has gotten into the habit of heading for the courts right after work. Bartholemew's enjoyment of the game is a force motivating him towards exercising; his aversion to out-of-shape fat is a force motivating him against not exercising, and the force of habit helps to maintain it all. Clearly, Bartholemew's willful intentions are not the sole force responsible for his successful exercise schedule. Indeed, his will alone might not be nearly strong enough to carry it out.

Bartholemew's success suggests that, when we think of the will as a weakish force, we can no longer give it *credit* for wholly determining our pro-intentional behavior. Similarly, we can no longer *blame* the will when we behave counterintentionally. Think again about Reginald, who found it impossible to get out of bed. Perhaps there were many forces contributing to his counterintentional behavior: he stayed up a little later than usual the night before; he was coming down with a cold; it was awfully cozy under the covers. It is more sensible to blame the *strength* of this combination of forces for Reginald's delinquency than the *weakness* of his will.

Recognizing the will as a weak force rather than a strong one makes it more understandable why counterintentional behavior happens so often. When counterintentional forces outdo our intention, it's because the counterintentional forces are *strong* compared to the normal weakness of the will, not because the will is *weak* compared to its usual strength. No wonder we so often find ourselves acting in ways we don't intend. And no wonder we can't fix that simply by trying harder.

Recognizing the will as weak force certainly makes us rethink our usual understandings of intentional *and* counterintentional behavior. However, as clarifications often do, it raises more questions as well. If my will is not top boss, what is? What are these stronger forces that influence me so much, and where do they come from? Can we map the "sources of forces?" Furthermore, if wills are weak, how can I be the master of my own behavior, the "captain of my soul?"

Sources of Forces

The picture painted so far is intriguing—and perhaps a little alarming as well. While the idea of a strong will puts us comfortably in control of our fate, the idea of a weak will casts us in a different role. Rather than rowing around the calm lake of life guided by reason, we find ourselves sailing an unwieldy vessel through a sea of troubles that pushes us here and there willy-nilly.

But wait. Comparing ourselves to a captain on the stormy sea suggests that we are in perpetual conflict with strong forces that compel our behavior. This simply is not the case. Much of the time, strong forces work together with, not contrary to, our best intentions. They produce the sort of conduct we genuinely want. The thirsty person seeks water; the especially thirsty person seeks it with vigor. What could be more appropriate? The person needs water to survive, and the force of strong thirst compels her to seek it out.

So let's not be too dismayed by the notion that strong forces more than willpower guide our behavior. Rather, we should be curious: Where do these strong forces come from? Why are they so strong? If we can map out some answers to these questions, we may be able to come to better terms with the forces that work upon us and through which we work upon the world.

So without any pretense at completeness, here's a brief survey of several common "sources of forces."

Primary Drives

First of all, we have to acknowledge the primary drives that shape our lives. We are biological organisms, inevitably concerned with survival and reproduction. To survive, we seek food and water. We protect ourselves with shelters. We stake out areas we claim as "ours" and defend them against encroachment. We fight or flee when danger threatens. To reproduce, we seek mates and care for and defend families.

Where do strong forces come from and why they are so strong?

In the case of primary drives, the answer seems plain. Such forces have evolved; they are so strong because they figure crucially in the continuation of the species. Any species without powerful motives of this sort would have died out long ago.

But what do such "tooth and claw" drives have to do with the relative comfort of urbane urban living? In comparatively prosperous contexts, do primary drives really influence the details of daily behavior? When basics such as food and shelter aren't lacking, don't people attend to loftier things?

Well, yes, to some extent. But strong and active primary drives can be seen at work in many aspects of everyday life. The sexual drive, for example, not only shapes our behavior as individuals but pervades our culture. Everything from the adolescent pangs celebrated in popular songs, to the popularity of romance literature, to the erotic care lavished on cars in advertisements show how lively this primal force remains. Other primary drives are equally pervasive and easily spotted.

Consider the sorts of entertainment that people find fulfilling. Sports, for example, often take the form of a kind of formalized combat. People, most often men, participate either as "warriors" or vicariously as spectators. Crime and adventure themes on television and in the movies also feed a hunger for the hunt and the battle. Or consider food and drink. We do need them to live— but we don't really need cocktails at 5:00, popcorn at the movies, hors d'oeuvres before dinner, and so on. Then why do we have them? Because primary drives connected with eating and nurturance permeate our social activities beyond the simple satisfaction of basic needs. The generalization seems to be this: Even when primary drives are basically pretty well satisfied, we still spend a lot of our time resatisfying them in yet more elaborate forms— nice meals, the pseudo-combat of sports, and so on.

Not only are primary drives strong factors in our everyday conduct—more so than we often give them credit for—but their strength is plainly and perniciously responsible for a good deal of counterintentional excess: eating too much, spending too loosely, fighting too easily, with no self-control. Such misbehavior, at least in part, reflects powerful primary drives which, although basically adaptive, become problematic when they so drastically overshoot the basic satisfaction of thirst, hunger or the need for integrity.

Why aren't primary drives better tuned? It's important to remember that for millions of years, human beings have evolved as a species under harsh conditions. In situations where basic survival is threatened, overshoot in primary drives is not a risk; you're lucky to get enough food or drink, modest protection for the night, a chance to raise your offspring to adulthood. Too *little* motivation is more of a risk than too much. Only strong primary drives allow us to cope with conditions of scarcity. So scarcity—whether real or perceived—engages our primary drives, and even in conditions of relative abundance we still experience the elaborated playing out of these drives, often causing no harm at all but sometimes resulting in counterintentional excess.

Force of Habit

We already think of habit as a force; we even speak of "the force of habit." What needs to be added here is that sometimes the force of habit can be strong indeed. Often we don't recognize this: if the habit is a positive or neutral one, we don't pit ourselves against it and so do not discover its strength. But suppose, for instance, that as a driver from the United States, you rent a car in England. Force of habit urges you to drive on the right. But the local laws—and the truck approaching you head-on in the right-hand lane!—tell you to drive on the left. You have to constantly suppress your old force of habit, and despite your vigilance, it may still get you into an accident.

Or, for another example from driving, suppose you go into a skid. The best strategy is to steer in the direction of the skid to regain traction. But force of habit from normal driving says to steer the other way, to straighten the car. It's very hard to act out of intention rather than out of habit in such urgent circumstances. Likewise, other behaviors that upon reflection we might like to change—for instance, excessive smoking or drinking—are in part sustained by the force of ingrained habit.

There's good reason why the mechanisms for habit formation yield habits of such strength. Habits stabilize our behavior. They allow us to act precisely and reliably without having to think moment to moment. This capacity to automatize our behavior gives us decided evolutionary advantages: What if, while running from tigers, cave dwellers had to deliberate about every step they took? Strong habit formation serves us well most of the time— so long as the behavior that gets habitualized serves us well.

But sometimes circumstances change, as with driving in England, and our habits become problematic. Moreover, the mechanism of habit formation works regardless of whether a behavior serves us well or not. So we develop habits that aren't necessarily in our best interests.

While some habits build up slowly through repetition or long experience, others form instantly from intense experiences. A trauma may create strong associations and behavioral reflexes that last for years. Suppose at the age of four you were bitten by an angry dog; you might be greatly frightened of dogs for the rest of your life. Whether habitual behavior develops slowly or instantly, it is characteristically *automatized* rather than *willful*, and occurs independently of our rational intentions.

And of course, just as some habits are too strong, some are too weak. Junior sort of brushes his teeth after every meal—about 70 percent of the time. You call your mom in Tucson more or less every week—more like every other week. It seems a human plight that habits are *not* necessarily well-tuned rational responses to situations. Some habits are stronger, some weaker, than circumstances warrant.

Physical Factors

Yet other strong forces derive from chemical and physical factors that affect the nervous system. Chemical reactions or irregularities, physical trauma, or even stress can powerfully influence our behavior. The force of will can be quite weak in comparison.

For a case in point, let's explore how addictive substances affect our behavior. Not just illegal drugs, but cigarettes and even coffee. The caffeine in coffee, for example, makes us wakeful and alert, actually improving performance on tasks that require attentiveness. But the body adapts to caffeine consumption, so that over time it needs more coffee for the same impact. That adaptation, in turn, means that withdrawal will bring uncomfortable symptoms—fatigue, headaches and irritability. Given the "pull" of wanting the alertness, plus the "push" of avoiding the withdrawal symptoms, no wonder addictive forces can be so strong.

Of course, you could say instead that coffee drinking is just another habit, like those discussed earlier. Coffee drinking *is* a habit and a good part of its momentum derives from that. But there is something special about habits like this. Coffee drinking is not merely a habit, like throwing your keys on the hall table when you walk in the door. The coffee drinking behavior is sustained day to day by the *chemical* push-pull effect described— unpleasant to quit and pleasant to continue.

Coffee has a relatively benign impact on the nervous system; cigarette smoking, for example, can do far more damage. Note that the general push-pull effect is the same: uncomfortable withdrawal symptoms if you quit that push you towards smoking, a short-term boost that pulls you towards smoking, and an adaptation of your physiology that requires you to consume more to get the same boost. A similar story can be told for alcohol and many other drugs. Of course, the complex and difficult topic of physical and psychological addiction merits more consideration than we give it here, but the push-pull model at least helps us to understand why chemical substances can influence us so strongly.

Direct physical trauma can also shape our conduct. Instances of injury to the brain through disease (such as Alzheimer's) or impact (such as a bonk on the head) can cause personality changes, erratic behavior, cognitive impairment, or a wide variety of other effects. A shocking case is that of Charles Whitman, a responsible, stable and commendable young man—who began to complain of headaches and odd feelings of hostility that neither his friends, his family, nor he himself could explain. His condition deteriorated rapidly until, one day, he took a rifle to the top of a tower overlooking the University of Texas campus and began to shoot at passersby, killing or wounding many of them. He was finally shot to death by the police. The autopsy revealed a tumor in the base of his brain, accounting for the uncharacteristic and tragic behavior.

Whitman's physical condition and ultimate behavior were extreme. But even in our *normal* functioning, we face physically-based forces like fatigue or stress that prompt reactions we never wanted: lack of concentration, inappropriate aggressiveness, emotional depression.

Any discussion of the physically-based influences on behavior raises interesting questions of the relationship between the mind and the body: To what extent is our psychological experience determined by physiological conditions? Or vice versa? Although these are not questions we expect to address in any depth here, we do recognize that the mind and the body are connected in intricate and powerful ways, physical factors are a source of powerful forces in determining our behavior, and our thoughts and attitudes influence our physical well-being.

Gangs of Forces

Forces can combine to yield a net result more powerful than any individual force, as in the chemical push-pull effect underlying much addictive behavior. Other push-pull effects abound in everyday life. For example, Lambert goes to a movie one night because he has heard good reviews of this film and because he wants to escape from some worrisome personal problems. He is pushed by his problems and pulled by the film.

Often a "gang" of several modest forces produces an over-whelming effect. And, when many forces recommend one action and only a few the opposite, it's usually *good* that the many forces prevail over the few.

For instance, suppose Audrey gets furious at the slowpoke driving in front of her. She has a sudden wild impulse to step on the pedal and put a dent in the slowpoke's bumper. But she comes nowhere near doing it. Why not? Look at the gang of counterforces at work. Audrey knows that a dent in the slow-poke's bumper means a corresponding dent in her bumper. Audrey fears a fight; perhaps the other driver is a maniac with a gun in the glove compartment! Audrey was well-conditioned by her parents to behave politely, not to mention legally. And she recognizes that the slowpoke is probably just trying to drive responsibly and isn't intentionally trying to inconvenience her. To be sure, in another individual the impulse might overwhelm such counterforces; sometimes drivers do dangerous impulsive things. But in general, such gangs of counterforces keep most of us behaving reasonably most of the time.

Unfortunately, sometimes gangs of forces keep us doing something we should not. Consider, for example, the force gang maintaining Enoch's overeating. First of all, Enoch has a strong habit of eating during certain leisure activities—reading or watching television. When he reads, he also eats. When he watches television, he also eats. Second, the sight of food compels him to eat, so a package of cookies left out on the kitchen counter will not last long. Third, Enoch eats to forget this or that problem, and even to forget about the miseries of feeling fat.

Fourth, Enoch has developed forces of rationalization to answer his guilt about overeating: "There's just a little bit left; why not finish it?" or "I haven't had this in a long time, so let me try it," or "I did a good job on the lawn; let me reward myself." Fifth, he responds physically to the force of basic salt and sugar cravings. Lastly, besides all this, Enoch has learned that dieting is a painful process with only meager success and embarrassing relapses. The history of failure creates a force against further efforts to cut back.

So no wonder Enoch stays overweight. A veritable gang of forces conspires to keep him eating. For Enoch to get healthy and stay healthy requires not just wrestling with any one of these forces but overcoming the whole gang.

In many cases like Enoch's, we can explain the powerful net force working toward or against something in terms of a gang of forces. The question remains why such gangs occur at all? Why is the "weather" of our motivational force system so immoderate?

One important factor to recognize is pure chance. Forces vary considerably from person to person and context to context. It is not surprising that occasionally forces coalesce into a gang simply by coincidence. For instance, Wally just happens to like the outdoors, enjoys the challenge of the hunt, savors peace and quiet rather than hiking about, wants to escape from some problems, has handy fishing sites not too far from home, and so on. So Wally becomes an ardent fisherman. Wally has discovered an activity—fishing—that happens to satisfy a bundle of forces that happen to be important to him.

Another factor to recognize is that gangs of forces develop over time. Consider the plight of Enoch again. Presumably Enoch did not initially eat in front of the television but learned that it was pleasant to do so. He did not start off with such rationalizing principles as "There's only a little bit left, so why not finish it?" but developed them to justify his overeating. He did not know at the outset that dieting is such a long tough haul but learned through his failed attempts. Likewise, Wally might have developed his various preferences and motivations through a number of other activities before he discovered fishing. In many such cases, a gang of forces forms not all at once, but over time. Through conditioning, elaboration of the behavior in question, and habit formation processes, the gang gets bigger and stronger.

Why Strong Forces Occur

We began by asking why so many strong forces seem to run wild in our psychological worlds. While at first this might have seemed puzzling, it has not been so hard to identify several reasons. Primary drives naturally operate as strong forces and, unfortunately, but understandably from an evolutionary perspective, often seem to overshoot their targets. Habits can become so ingrained that they function as strong forces in shaping our behavior. The characteristic push-pull effect associated with various minor or major chemical addictions keeps us entrenched in conducts we might prefer to drop. Other physically-based influences—from disease or injury to simple fatigue—directly influence us and our conduct. Finally, groups of independent forces gang up, either by chance or developmentally, to influence our behavior with great power in some particular direction.

These and other mechanisms that might account for strong forces are distinctly doubled-edged. Most of the time they work for us, reinforcing our best intentions and giving us the energy to do as we will. But sometimes they undermine our best intentions, pressing us to behave in counterintentional ways. Thus they sometimes block us out of behaviors our best intentions recommend, or block us into behaviors our best intentions tell us to avoid.

Dodging Strong Forces: Blocked In

It seems that strong forces stalk our psychological world, coercing us to follow their command. To be sure, most of the time these strong forces may work more for us than against us. But this is not always so, or counterintentional behavior would not be the problem that it is. Not only are strong forces about, but the force of the will against them is weaker than we usually imagine. "Muscling through" the problem by sheer will power most often does not work. So what recourse is left when just trying harder fails?

Enoch changes his environment. Consider Enoch again, "blocked in" by bad eating habits. The ice cream in the refrigerator is a perpetual lure. When Enoch wanders through the kitchen for any reason, the box of cookies or bag of potato chips on the shelf snares his attention. When Enoch sits down for an evening of television, each commercial signals a dash to the refrigerator. Encoh tells himself he should cut down, and sometimes he does for a day or two. But the fact is that the forces are just too strong for him. What can he do?

Instead of changing himself, Enoch changes the situation. First of all, he keeps food out of sight. If there are snack items about, they go in the cupboard, not out on the counter. He recruits the cooperation of his wife and children in seeing that they *stay* in the cupboard. Secondly, he arranges for many items simply not to be around. At his request, no more ice cream is purchased and diet soda takes the place of the sugar variety. The kids like cookies, but now his wife buys only the kinds that Enoch does not care for. With the help of these and some other tactics, Enoch slims down.

What lessons can be drawn from Enoch's experience? Enoch had a problem with forces too strong to "muscle" with his will, but he found a way to dodge the forces. There were steps he did have enough will power to take—asking his family's help in keeping food out of sight, not purchasing certain foods, and so on. Enoch did not change his psychology; he still likes ice cream just as much as ever and, if it's around, he would eat just as impulsively as ever. Instead, Enoch applied his will to modifying his environment. Enoch might have picked up this trick from reading a book on dieting problems with a behaviorist perspective; a standard behaviorist move is to control yourself through controlling the environment. Even though weight problems are often complex, and what worked for Enoch might not work as well for others, manipulating the environment can often be a surprisingly effective means of controlling the influence of powerful forces.

Penny changes her perceptions. Consider another case of being "blocked in" to a behavior. Penny, a college freshmen at a demanding university, finds herself blocked into a cycle of work that leaves no time for relaxation and creates a feeling of spiraling pressure and anxiety. Penny consults with a therapist on the staff of the university about her problem. She complains that there seems to be no time for everything in a single day. Sure, she can snatch an occasional hour to unwind, but, she complains, "it's all so crammed into too little time." She longs for a more calm and regular approach to existence.

The therapist and Penny work out an interesting solution: Penny will think of each *two* days as *one* day. Thinking in a two-day cycle (with a "nap" at "noon"), she will have more total time to organize in an orderly fashion with plenty of room in a "day" for her multiple studies and some serious recreation too. Penny finds the "two days as one" model liberating, because the larger chunk of time proves easier to organize.

Notice the contrast between Penny and Enoch. Enoch actually changed his environment to change how he felt and acted. But Penny simply thought about her same old environment in a different way to change how she felt and acted. Yet the two cases

75

share something as well. Like Enoch, Penny changed by doing something she *could* do, abandoning something she could not. Penny could not directly set aside her feelings of stress and her restless anxious behavior, but she *could* think about her environment in a new way. Therapists often call such a reorganization of experience a *reframing*: by seeing a situation in a new way, you invoke a different array of forces that you can live with more comfortably.

Forrest changes the forces. Here is yet another example, different in some ways and yet similar in others. Forrest is an alcoholic, "blocked in" by his craving for alcohol. Forrest wants to quit, but, counter to his best intention, he cannot seem to get himself to do so. Forrest follows a course adopted by many others; he joins Alcoholics Anonymous and finds there the support he needs. In force terms, Forrest has done something different from both Enoch and Penny, but exactly what? To be sure, like Enoch, he has changed his environment somewhat: now he goes to AA meetings. But he can't entirely avoid environmental temptations; he still walks past the same bars on the way home from work. Like Penny, he has changed the way he perceives the circumstances somewhat: attendance at AA helps him to identify himself publicly as an alcoholic. Yet his feelings haven't really changed; the bar he passes exerts its pull and a drink still seems like a great end to the day.

These changes in the world Forrest encounters and perceives account for some of his progress, but more importantly, Forrest has added to the forces at play. Now he feels responsible to the AA group. He reports his triumphs and his difficulties to them. His lapses let them down and his successes win their approval. He develops a trusting relationship with his AA "sponsor." It is these factors more than anything else that keep him on the wagon. You might say that new forces have been recruited into the situation to help Forrest manage better the old forces. Despite this contrast with the tactics of Enoch and Penny, again there is a similarity. While Forrest cannot just stop drinking by an act of will, he beats the problem by doing something else he *can* get himself to do: in this case, attend AA meetings.

Rhea changes her reactions. A final example rounds out this array of ways to dodge strong forces. Rhea has a quick temper and all too often finds herself telling people off, sometimes unjustifiably and, even more frequently, imprudently. After a couple of rows with her boss, Rhea even finds herself at risk for her job. Rhea realizes that she needs to control her temper better, but how? She tries simply to suppress her anger when it occurs, but the anger will not go away; it keeps rising as inevitably as the tide, and lands her in trouble again.

Rhea finally adopts the classic remedy for a quick temper: counting to ten under your breath. Only Rhea decides she had better count to twenty. To her own surprise, Rhea finds that beginning her count at the first sign of rising ire makes quite a difference. By the time she reaches twenty, she feels as though she has passed the peak of her anger, and she often manages what before would have been unthinkable: dropping the bone of contention altogether.

Rhea's tactic in one respect resembles the strategies of Enoch, Penny and Forrest: Rhea cannot directly change her behavior by an act of will. But she can do something else—count to twenty. By doing this something else, she dodges the strong force and gets the result she wants. In other ways, though, her tactic is quite different from Enoch, Penny and Forrest. She does not change the world she encounters: she still runs into upsetting situations with her usual circle of co-workers and friends. Nor does her perception of events change: she still finds many things that people say and do stupid or offensive. Nor does she recruit new forces into the situation, for instance, by making promises to her family or friends. Rather, Rhea changes her immediate behavior in a way that modifies the forces at work. Basically, she distracts herself by the counting, a detached activity that works counter to the mood of the anger and also simply gives the anger time to abate.

In summary, the general maneuver that Enoch, Penny, Forrest and Rhea have in common might be called "strategic use of the will." The four faced similar problems: as in any case of counter-intentional behavior, none of them could get themselves to do directly what their best intentions recommended. The forces at play simply were too strong for sheer will power to overcome. But in each case, there was something else they could get themselves to do that helped them to manage the strong forces.

Of course, nothing guarantees that what worked for Enoch, Penny, Forrest and Rhea would work for everyone. Problems of counterintentional behavior can be extremely complex and deep-rooted. Nonetheless, almost as a point of logic, solutions to such problems *have* to involve doing things you *can* do that, by way of side effects, change your situation. You use the will strategically, to outmaneuver the forces at work, rather than directly, to muscle the forces at work.

Dodging Strong Forces: Blocked Out

We've illustrated the *strategic use of the will* with several examples of "blocked in." The following scenario makes a similar point for "blocked out." In addition, the example demonstrates how the different strategies of Enoch, Penny, Forrest and Rhea can be combined to recruit a number of *pro*-intentional forces into a gang that pushes your behavior in a better direction.

Desmond is a doctoral candidate experiencing problems of momentum with his thesis, as so many do. He has managed to get started but cannot seem to maintain much enthusiasm or make much progress, however hard he tries. Desmond is "blocked out" of what his best intentions recommend—getting on with his thesis.

With some help from a counselor, Desmond mounts a concerted attack on his problem. First of all, Desmond modifies his working environment and schedule. He invests $100 in a new desk and hangs favorite prints around it. He buys tapes of non-intrusive music to enjoy while he does some of his more boring and routine thesis work, like alphabetizing his files.

On top of that, Desmond reframes his perception of his thesis. He has been thinking about it basically as a rite of passage you need to get through. Now he thinks about it as the platform for later professional work. The thesis could become several articles, or the basis for a book. Desmond starts to reconfigure somewhat his plan for the organization of the thesis with publications in mind. It may even take a little longer to complete that way, Desmond thinks. But the payoffs warrant some extra effort! Now the thesis seems more worthwhile than it did simply as an obstacle to overcome on the way to a degree.

Desmond also joins a thesis support group comprised of students with similar dilemmas. The group meets once every two weeks and the half-dozen participants share their experiences, frustrations and tactics. Desmond feels sustained by the encouragement of others in the group and feels he owes it to the group to keep moving and so reinforce their efforts as well. Like Forrest

79

through his attendance at Alcoholics Anonymous meetings, Desmond has recruited new forces to give him momentum through his association with the thesis support group.

Finally, Desmond teaches himself fresh reactions to the barriers he still sometimes encounters when meaning to sit down and work on his thesis. For instance, in order to counteract the anxiety he invariably experiences, Desmond makes a deal with himself: He will just sit down at his desk, but he will not start work. He will read a mystery novel for a bit. Then, after a few minutes, already sitting there, he will turn to his thesis. Once he is sitting in place, in an alert but relaxed frame of mind, Desmond finds it easier to get deeply involved in his dissertation.

One more example of the strategic use of the will bears mentioning, simply for its charm and elegance. A colleague told us of her high school track coach who found himself in charge of an enthusiastic but undisciplined freshman team. His students were eager to improve their skills and stamina, and they felt committed to maintaining their daily training schedule between practices. They fully intended to follow through on this commitment. Yet at each practice they sheepishly confessed that they had failed to put in their required miles. They were as frustrated as the coach; they just could not seem to make themselves do their laps every day, despite their best intentions and sincere promises. They bemoaned their pitiful lack of will power. They were blocked out.

The coach resolved the problem in an elegant way by changing the requirements slightly. Instead of asking the students to run their laps every day, he requested only that they get suited up every day. They did not have to run at all if they did not want to, so long as they donned their running gear, sneakers and all. It took a while for the coach to convince his students that he was serious, but finally they all agreed to institute the new policy. The students found that, compared to the grueling running schedule, merely getting suited up was a much more manageable commitment, one that they had little trouble meeting. Moreover, once they were suited up, running some laps did not look so bad, even though they did not have to. In fact, it seemed kind of silly simply to get back into street clothes without taking advantage of being suited up. Before long, the students were training diligently every day between practices.

The coach's way of handling this situation takes strategic advantage of the limited will power his students had at their disposal. In particular, the coach's tactic resembles Rhea's move in substituting counting to twenty for her usual reaction of losing her temper, as well as Desmond's in sitting down at his desk to read, and then perhaps to work on his thesis. In this case, the coach recognized that the agonies of a workout on top of the nuisance of suiting up were just too much to overcome. But divide and conquer! His students had the will power to suit up—if they did not feel that they had to run. And they had the will power to run—if they were already suited up.

A Circle of Causation

The moral of these tales is that there are many ways to use the will strategically. Enoch changed his environment; Penny changed how she perceived her situation; Forrest recruited new forces to help him deal with his problem; Rhea undercut her usual reactions by substituting a different reaction. Desmond, struggling with his thesis, adopted all four tactics. And the coach employed only the fourth in a particularly ingenious way.

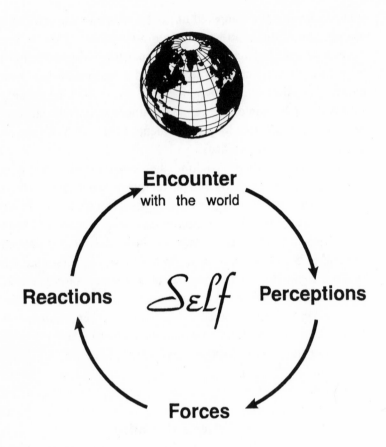

Circle of Causation

To generalize, we can see in these examples four different natural intervention points for the strategic use of the will in coping with strong forces. Taken together, the four intervention points form what you might call a ''circle of causation.'' We can diagram it as on the previous page.

For example, imagine Rhea facing one of those situations that provokes her temper. How does her loss of temper come about? Reading clockwise from the top, first of all she encounters a situation—say someone makes a joke in poor taste. This gives rise to certain perceptions—''this person is being rude to me.'' This in turn gives rise to certain forces—*anger*. The forces in turn ignite an overt reaction—loss of temper. If one wants to follow the circle further, Rhea's reaction presumably modifies the situation—the joker, who happens to be her boss, takes offense at her reaction. This creates a new encounter, a new perception, new forces, and so on.

While this model is rather rough-and-ready, it makes a crucial point about our actions and feelings. They do not emanate solely from forces or any other single step in the circle. Rather they are the product of the whole circle. What you encounter, how you perceive it, what forces get evoked, how you react, and how that reaction changes the situation leading to a new encounter, all figure in your overall actions and feelings.

The model thereby says something of great importance about counterintentional behavior. It is not just strong forces that do the mischief; it is the circle of causation, which sometimes becomes a ''vicious circle'' that keeps us trapped in patterns of actions and feelings contrary to our best intentions.

The circle of causation offers an ample and dynamic understanding of how counterintentional behavior occurs, and it also offers the leverage of multiple opportunities. Exactly because the circle involves four links (encounter, perception, forces, reaction), it offers a chance to intervene in the operation of strong forces by breaking the circle at any one of the four (as did Enoch, Penny, Forrest and Rhea, respectively). Or you can make a concerted attack on the four, as did Desmond. In fact, for stubborn problems, there is a lot to be said for Desmond's attack on all fronts.

The circle of causation can be used to categorize many standard therapeutic techniques, revealing something about their basic tactics. For instance, systematic desensitization is a method employed to help people with many phobias. If you are afraid of spiders enough to want to get rid of the fear, a therapist may ask you first just to think about spiders and relax physically, then actually look at a spider from a distance and relax physically, then approach closer and relax physically, then stand very close and relax physically, then touch the web and relax physically. Gradually you become very good at being calm in the presence of spiders. How does this fit the circle? A survey of the circle's four parts suggests that this tactic works on reactions, substituting one reaction to the forces for another. The phobic individual cannot just make the fear go away. But, strategically applying the will, the phobic individual *can* physically relax in the (not too close) presence of the feared object. Since panic and physical relaxation are mutually exclusive, this reaction begins a change in the ongoing cycle of causation that progresses and continues until spiders no longer trigger panic.

Also, therapists often work with clients to help them to view their circumstances in new ways. Through such reframing, what was seen as a problem can sometimes be reconceived as an opportunity, what was seen as a personal weakness can be reconceived as a very general human foible, and so on. Where does this fit the circle? It amounts to remaking the perceptions of an encounter.

For yet another example, therapists may work with clients to help them to reorganize their daily lives. A therapist might suggest to a couple, "Avoid talk about family finances except for an 'official' time during the week, because the two of you will just end up arguing." Where does such a maneuver fit the circle? It shapes the world encounter. For one more example, therapists may involve other family members or support groups, and may help clients to see their dilemmas in relation to other aspects of their lives to which no connections have been made before. Where does this fit? It recruits new forces into the situations that may support the clients' efforts to change.

Of course, a particular therapeutic move often fits more than one of the four categories. This should neither surprise nor dismay us. First of all, many therapeutic moves work in more than one way at the same time, so they ought to match more than one step around the circle of causation. Second, inevitably the borderlines between such broad categories are somewhat fuzzy. But that's okay. To be useful, an organizer like the circle doesn't have to classify *everything* neatly so long as it helps us to sort things out most of the time.

So "official" therapeutic tactics can be seen in terms of strategic use of the will and classified into the circle of causation. But the circle isn't just for formal therapeutic contexts. Both the strategic use of the will and tactics at any point in the circle occur routinely in everyday life, far from the professional therapist's office and the concerns that bring people there. Like force theory itself, strategic use of the will and the intervention points in the circle of causation are implicit in the ways many people cope with the minor problems of life.

For instance, do you have trouble getting up in the morning? When you set an alarm clock, you are modifying the environment you encounter. Do you find that you reach over, turn off the alarm, and go back to sleep? When you place the alarm clock further away, so you cannot as easily silence it, you are modifying the environment again.

On weekend mornings, when you do not set the alarm, do you find it hard to get out of bed and feel guilty for loafing in bed? That game where you put one foot out from under the sheets first, which somehow then drags the rest of you behind it, is a case of substituting a reaction you can make for one you cannot: Although the forces say ''lie there'' and you cannot just spring into action, you *can* put your foot out. Or perhaps you remind yourself of the fun project you planned for the morning, in which case you are bringing additional forces to bear. Or perhaps you reconceive your situation—''I *deserve* to lie in bed for another hour considering the week I put in''—and go back to sleep. You have reframed the situation and, up or not, you are enjoying yourself.

Deep Causes of Block

The similarity between how people handle minor foibles and many professional psychotherapeutic techniques is striking. To be sure, the popular image of therapy is that problems of block and related psychological problems are always ''deep.'' They reflect indirect causes buried in one's childhood memories and demand mysterious treatments to bring the forces to light and change them.

But this is a very misleading picture of both therapy and the human condition, a picture that itself needs reframing. Many problems of block are not particularly deep at all! They are quite transparent: matters of forces that we recognize perfectly well and that, unfortunately, happen to be strong enough to produce conduct contrary to our best intentions. Such forces do not so much need to be unveiled as outmaneuvered. And, as the circle of causation shows, there are many prospects for outmaneuvering mischievous forces.

None of this is to say that there are no deep problems. There certainly are. Indeed, we devote most of the rest of this book to exploring the complexities and subtleties of block. The point, rather, is that there are plenty of "surface" problems, too. Moreover, sometimes surface tactics can solve a deep problem. Even though the historical roots of your spider phobia or your quick temper may be dark and mysterious, very often systematic desensitization or counting to twenty will help to handle the problem and bring about substantive changes in both your behavior and your feelings.

It is worth wondering why deep explanations of psychological dilemmas sometimes lure us into complicated labyrinths of interpretation and speculation when more straightforward explanations would serve better. Let's do a force analysis! We are attracted by such deep explanations for a number of reasons: First of all, a deep explanation is simply more interesting, just as a duck-billed platypus is more interesting than a duck or a fish. Second, our mistaken belief in the will as a strong force tends to promote depth explanations, because we assume that something deep must be going on to overwhelm a strong will. Third, a deep explanation helps us to avoid responsibility and shame in the face of our own inability to behave as we intend. We can sum it all up in an example: If you cannot keep your hands out of the chocolates because you are a habitual eater with a chocolate craving, how dull this is and what hard work you'll have to do to resist temptation. But if, down deep, you are punishing your parents by overeating and at the same time punishing yourself for punishing them, well, how *interesting*, and, at the same time, no wonder you feel helplessly in the grip of powerful forces.

Again, we don't mean to suggest that deep explanations are never appropriate or accurate. Clearly they often are. But we should also be leery of our preference for deep explanations, since other factors may well be influencing this preference: for instance, the lure of the exotic and the way deep explanations protect our belief in a strong will and excuse our behavior. Ironically, since these are factors that people are often unaware of, we are suggesting here a deep explanation for why deep explanations are often deceptively attractive! To explore the depths even more deeply, in the next chapter we turn from *strong* forces to *hidden* forces.

ThinkAbouts

*What does all this mean to you? How might you continue
to think about the ideas presented in this chapter?*

• When you find yourself counterintentionally ''blocked in'' or
''blocked out,'' you'll likely berate yourself for having ''no will
power.'' But remember that the will is probably not as a strong a
force as you expect it to be.

• You may still want to beat yourself up for being a weak-willed
wimp. Instead, take a moment to evaluate your situation and
identify the strong forces—*besides* your will power or lack of
it—that *are* producing your counterintentional behavior.

• Try drawing a ''circle of causation'' describing your particular
situation. What do you encounter? What are your perceptions?
What forces are aroused? How do you react? You may be able to
change your behavior by intervening at one or more of these
points in the cycle.

• Remember that what you can't do by sheer will power alone,
you may well be able to accomplish with a *strategic application*
of the will. That is, even if you can't directly correct your
problematic behavior by an act of will, you may be able to affect
it *in*directly by strategically manipulating the circle of causation.

Chapter 3

MYSTERIOUSLY BLOCKED
The Role of Hidden Forces

Edgar tucks the covers up around his son, Edgar Junior, as they settle down for a bedtime story. This is a favorite moment of the day for both of them, when they feel especially close and happy. Tonight, the boy looks forward to finishing, at last, the storybook that they've been reading together for several weeks. But, as Edgar begins to read aloud, a feeling of sadness overcomes him. At a poignant moment in the chapter, his eyes fill with tears. He fights to maintain composure, but finds he can't go on. His son, concerned, asks, "Dad, what's the matter?" Edgar is at a loss to explain. He makes a hasty excuse, ending their storytime early without finishing the book.

For several evenings after, Edgar makes more excuses to avoid spending time with his son, especially at bedtime. No one in the family can understand his strange behavior. Then Edgar receives a phone call from his sister, Ethel. In the course of their conversation, she reminds him that the following day is the anniversary of their own father's death. As they continue to talk, Edgar realizes that he has strong and unresolved feelings about this important loss—feelings that have now unexpectedly reemerged and shaped his recent mood and behavior. Quite unintentionally, Edgar has been avoiding his son in order to avoid his own painful feelings about his father and his father's death.

Hidden forces—that's what seems to be going on in Edgar's case. And with all of us, perhaps many undetected forces contribute to our conduct. There is something intriguing about the notion of hidden forces, as though they prove the complexity of our psyches or the depth of our emotions. But does it make sense, this notion that forces can be hidden? How can a force hide?

Hidden existence. First, the very existence of any force might be hidden. Suppose Edgar's wife asks him to explain how come he's neglecting his son. Edgar reacts with unconcern, "Oh, I dunno, Junior's probably been busy lately." Here, Edgar recognizes that he hasn't seen much of Junior but doesn't seem to think that this calls for any special explanation. The existence of a force is hidden even though Edgar acknowledges the situation it produced. Or suppose the same query from his wife gets the response, "Me? I'm not neglecting Junior! Why would I neglect Junior?" Here, Edgar doesn't even recognize his odd behavior; the force is hidden because the work it has done has gone unnoticed. In such cases, forces stay hidden because people don't see any reason to look for them.

Hidden Strength. Second, it's sometimes not so much the existence of a force that is hidden from us as its strength. For example, in another twist of Edgar's tale, suppose that Edgar knows quite well that this week is the anniversary of his father's death. He recognizes some painful feelings. But, underestimating their strength, he doesn't think of them as an explanation for his neglecting Junior. In general, we often underestimate the ability of strong forces to shape our behavior. (It's worth noting that hiddenness and strength are separate matters. Strong forces are not necessarily hidden and hidden forces are not necessarily strong.)

Hidden nature. Third, the nature of a force can be hidden. For example, Edgar might notice his odd behavior towards his son, but blame it on the current stress of his job. Here he has a straightforward and fairly plausible force explanation that masks the "real" force at work. Of course, we needn't make an either/or choice between an "overwork" explanation and a "grief" explanation for Edgar's behavior. Both can be involved. But the more powerful factor, his grief, is hidden behind a more every-day factor, stress.

While the notion of hidden forces helps us to understand Edgar's plight, the notion also brings up a pile of problems. Identifying hidden forces can be tricky. It's easy to call upon hidden forces not only to explain the otherwise inexplicable but to excuse the otherwise inexcusable: "The Devil made me do it!" And, even if one is not a scoundrel, one may well be a dupe—the notion that hidden forces underlie our behavior casts us as oblivious pawns, ignorant of our own motivations, subject to forces we don't even see. With hidden forces running around, how responsible are we for our own behavior?

Moreover, when we posit forces that by definition are hidden, what makes us sure they're "really" there? Who's to say? And why would we even want to hypothesize hidden forces to explain anything?

Why Hidden Forces?

When you have eliminated the impossible, whatever remains, however improbable, must be the truth.

—Sherlock Holmes

In some ways, we are all quite used to the notion of hidden forces. One cultural legacy of Freud and other 19th century psychological theorists is the idea that intrapsychic forces *of which we are not conscious* shape our attitudes and conduct—Oedipal urges, repressed jealousies, or whatever. The unconscious lurks within us like a troll under a bridge, ready to jump out, commit some peculiar and distasteful act, and hop back before we really get a good look at it.

Even if you know nothing about Freud, chances are you are still quite familiar with the idea that the human mind consists of both conscious and unconscious psychic mechanisms. Indeed, you may be so used to the concept of hidden forces, that you've never noticed what a radical notion it really is.

Let's try to shake off for a moment our familiarity with the idea of hidden forces long enough to ask, "Who needs 'em?" After all, it's generally not that difficult to identify what forces shape our behavior. We drink because we are thirsty, eat because we are hungry, scratch because we itch. To posit the existence of hidden forces just brings into play a whole range of mysterious entities much less connected to our direct experience.

An analogy makes clearer how bold a step it really is to posit the existence of hidden forces. Imagine a murder mystery where several characters have good reason to do in the rich and imperious Gavin Pottle. His wife suspects he is cheating on her. He has been embezzling funds from his best friend and financial advisor. He has argued with Bradford, longtime butler for the Pottle family, threatening to cut the butler's stipend out of his will. Yet despite all these obvious suspects, Inspector Persimmon of Scotland Yard insists that a mysterious stranger committed the crime. How odd! Think of hidden forces as mysterious strangers: Why suggest them when visible forces will do as well? Why take seriously the notion of hidden forces?

Well, to retell the tale of Gavin Pottle, suppose that Pottle was thoroughly devoted to his wife, he was the best friend his best friend ever had, and five witnesses say the butler was drinking at the neighborhood pub at the time of the crime. Moreover, the modus operandi of the crime matches perfectly that of several other crimes recently committed in the neighborhood. Then, while wife, friend, or butler *might* have done the dirty deed, the hypothesis of a mysterious stranger becomes more plausible. To generalize the point, we think of hidden factors when they help make sense of things that visible factors don't account for.

So instead of the case of Gavin Pottle, take the case of Edgar and Edgar Junior that opened this chapter. Edgar's distanced behavior from his son shows no direct connection to the anniversary of his father's death. He does not even remember the death at first. Yet, how else to account for Edgar's behavior? Edgar certainly seems to love his son. Nothing obvious happened to explain his sudden reticence. The usual suspects are rounded up and dismissed as improbable culprits. So it makes sense to propose a mysterious stranger, a hidden force.

Although Edgar's circumstances are unusual and striking, we do well to recognize that we routinely turn to hidden forces to account for our behavior. For instance, it's not uncommon to realize that you've been angry or jealous without knowing it. Suppose Mildred snaps at Patrick out of the blue, without understanding why. Later, in a moment of reflection, Mildred makes sense of it all: "Oh, I was *angry* at Patrick," or "Oh yes, I was *jealous* of Patrick." But why does Mildred pick covert anger or jealously specifically? Presumably because anger or jealousy

95

accounts for her overt behavior; she acted in an angry or jealous way, and sees reasons later why she might have felt angry or jealous, even though she didn't recognize those feelings at the time.

In other words, hidden forces are like a detective's or a scientist's hypotheses: We do not find them obvious—if we did, we would not call them "hidden." Rather, we deduce them in order to explain behavior that otherwise would be mysterious. When we lack a surface explanation, and the hidden force we propose makes sense of the circumstances, we feel confident in the hypothesis.

As with any interpretive enterprise, the ultimate justification for positing a hidden force lies in how well the hypothesis plays out: How neatly and thoroughly does it account for the behavior in question? How well does it continue to do so as further behavior unfolds? From this perspective, the question, "Are hidden forces really there?" has a straightforward answer. We say that they are "really there"—just as we say atoms, electrons and quarks are "really there"—when the hypothesis holds up well.

Why Do Forces Get Hidden?

Edgar's attitude towards his son reflected his feelings about his father's death—feelings that played a hidden role in his behavior. But what about Edgar's sister, Ethel, and her own grief about their father's death? Suppose that, like Edgar, Ethel also had a tough week. She found herself thinking often about their father and even went up to her attic on impulse to pull out some old family photos. Looking at them made her cry. She telephoned

Edgar for company in her grief on this important anniversary.

Edgar and Ethel both mourned their father's death. Ethel recognized her grief and its influence, while for Edgar, this force was hidden. What a puzzling difference! Perhaps Ethel can tolerate difficult emotions, while Edgar can't. Or maybe Edgar usually experiences grief quite openly, but just not this time. In either case, we have to wonder why. How come in one situation a force works out in the open, while in another situation the same force goes into hiding? How and why do forces *get* hidden?

Hidden by Accident

In exploring the hows and whys of hidden forces, it's important to recognize that forces occasionally get hidden by accident. Although this may not describe Edgar's situation, forces sometimes escape our attention for no other reason than random cognitive error.

Take for example Ruby, who is not only a conscientious student but also an excellent typist. This skill is a good thing since Ruby types on a cantankerous old Olivetti and mistakes always mean messy white-out and useless delays. One night, Ruby is typing the final version of a term paper from her handwritten notes, editing and rewriting as she goes along. She has been at it for several hours and has been getting increasingly impatient with the whole process. For the past two or three pages she seems to have spent an inordinate amount of time correcting one typo after another. She finally lets out a groan of frustration, "What's the *matter* with me?" Ruby's roommate calls from her side of the room, "For heaven's sake, you're probably too tired."

"Oh," Ruby says. "Of *course* I'm too tired. Too tired even to see how tired I am!'' She straightens her papers and gets up from her desk. After a short coffee break with her roommate, she returns to her typing with a renewed alertness and sense of control.

In situations like Ruby's, a force at work gets hidden from us only in the sense that our attention has been occupied elsewhere. In general, we only have the time, energy and cognitive capacity to attend to a few particularly relevant matters. Usually, this is all we really need to do to get by. But not always.

When forces do get hidden through random error, the casual counsel of others can be very helpful. We may be puzzled by our odd or counterintentional behavior until a friend or spouse—for Ruby it was her roommate—points out to us a side of our situation that escaped our notice. And then the puzzle is solved. It's like being stuck on a math problem until a tutor points out a simple error: ''You forgot to square X, didn't you?'' In such situations, we aren't blocked for any deep reason.

So forces can get hidden by accident. But this doesn't mean that we have to depend on the lucky accident of a friend's input to disclose them! Our ability to detect and to avoid such errors is, at least to some extent, a *learned* skill. With math or behavior problems alike, it's a useful problem-solving strategy to pause every now and then to scan the field for the presence of overlooked factors. We can train ourselves to ask, as a matter of routine, ''Are things going as I expect? Have I overlooked anything?'' In this way, we can catch ourselves in our own trivial errors and straighten them out.

Hidden by Design

When a force gets hidden by accident, we think of it as an innocent mistake. But when Sigmund claims that his dentist appointment simply slipped his mind, we can't help but wonder

98

. . . Is his mistake really such an innocent one? Consider the following cartoon:

SHERMAN ON THE MOUNT by Lee and Fruchey

What makes this cartoon funny? Certainly more than cognitive accident is at work here. We see right away that Sherman's prospective diet generates in him avoidant stay-in-bed forces, and that these forces explain his initially puzzling behavior. More than accident or error hides these forces from him. He doesn't want to start his diet, doesn't want to admit he doesn't want to start his diet, in fact doesn't even want to think about starting his diet. As with Sherman so with us all: forces sometimes get hidden not by accident but by *design*.

Hidden by design—an intriguing notion. Let's think some more about Sherman and his diet. What sense does it make for the forces in his situation to be hidden? The look on his face gives us a clue. He seems quite cozy and blissful as long as he's unaware of the "real" force at work; even the bird sings merrily. Sure, he's puzzled by his counterintentional behavior, but at least he's comfortable. As soon as his friend reminds him that today he starts his diet, he becomes quite miserable. Functionally, then, the force hides to save him from pain, albeit only temporarily. The pain it saves him from is the stress he experiences when his get-out-of-bed-and-start-dieting forces clash with his stay-in-bed-and-avoid-dieting counterforces.

99

So let's generalize. When a force encounters a barrier or counterforce, there results a real or potential conflict that causes us distress. To save us the pain of an overt conflict, a force often plays itself out indirectly, so its identity gets hidden from us.

This describes Edgar's experience perfectly. He had many strong and painful feelings about his father and his father's death—grief, anger, sadness. These became acute in the presence of his son, repelling him. This repellant force could not play itself out openly because it encountered counterforces—Edgar's love for his son and desire to be with him. There could be other unrecognized counterforces at work, as well—perhaps a subtle sense of pride on Edgar's part that grown men mustn't cry, or an unacknowledged feeling of shame that he hadn't yet recovered from his father's death, or a quiet fear that he might be overwhelmed if he allowed himself to feel the full extent of his grief.

So the forces that determine our behavior don't always do so simply by "winning out" among all the forces at work in a straightforward way. If they did, Edgar would simply accept his grief, and Sherman would simply admit that he doesn't want to diet. Instead, it seems that forces operate covertly, determining our behavior while avoiding overt and painful conflicts with the barriers or counterforces that stand in their way.

And why do some forces hide and others not, or why might a force hide at some times and not at others? The examples of Edgar and Sherman suggest this: forces hidden by design are those forces that, were we to experience them directly, would arouse in us painfully negative reactions. They would shock us, or dismay us, or disgust us, or frighten us. Sherman's good conscience makes the overt expression of his anti-diet feelings unacceptable to him. Perhaps for Edgar, the overt acknowledgement of his grief would arouse in him painful feelings of shame

100

and fear as well as sadness. In general, it seems that forces get hidden when we find them too painful to look at.

Talking about hidden forces this way raises a question: how is it that we can hide things from our*selves*. If Sherman is hiding his *own* thoughts or feelings from him*self*, it would seem that there is more than one Sherman! Who is the real Sherman and how much does he know? A later chapter, Chapter 5, looks at the concept of the self and explores the implications of our capacity to have thoughts and feelings *about* our own thoughts and feelings.

Mechanisms by Which Forces Hide

Even when we are aware that forces can hide, and even when we are on the lookout for them, hidden forces can still be difficult to spot. One reason is that forces can hide in several ways. Turning from the "why" to the "how" of hidden forces, let's take a look at some of these mechanisms in action.

Avoidance. Ignatious is thrilled about his soon-to-be announced engagement to his girlfriend, Tamara. Although he's been feeling increasingly edgy recently, he figures it's nothing—after all, everyone knows he and Tamara are the perfect match. Then one evening Tamara asks him, "Iggy, dear, is something wrong? You've been acting a little testy lately." Since there *isn't* really anything wrong, he simply replies, "No, nothing's wrong."

Now Ignatious is usually a very chatty guy. This curt response is unusual. So Tamara persists: "Iggy, honeybunch, if something's wrong, I'd like to talk about it." Not really having anything to say, Ignatious replies, "Honestly, Tamara, nothing's wrong." Finally, Tamara says, "Iggy, sweetie-pie, I know something's wrong. Are you angry at me?" To which Iggy snaps back, "I am *not* angry! AND QUIT CALLING ME BABY NAMES!!''

What's going on with Ignatious? He has been feeling and acting angry, but he doesn't recognize anger as a force determining his behavior—even when Tamara tries to ask him about it. There may be any number of reasons why Ignatious is testy to begin with; perhaps there are things about Tamara that bother him more than he can admit, or perhaps he's angry at Tamara's mother for her strong opinions about the wedding plans. Likewise, there may be any number of reasons why it is unacceptable for him to recognize his own anger; he could be afraid that his anger, if it were expressed, would hurt Tamara or drive her away. Regardless of the reasons, Ignatious's anger cannot play itself out in an acceptable way, so he simply *avoids* acknowledging its existence. He denies both to himself and to Tamara that he's angry at all, even as he loses his temper.

So let's call this mechanism *avoidance*. In cases of *avoidance*, a force that cannot play itself out in an acceptable way simply isn't acknowledged. We've seen that Iggy's avoidance perhaps causes more problems than it solves, but sometimes avoidance can be a very positive mechanism. It has its adaptive benefits. For example, imagine that Lilly, who is an excellent driver, hits a slick spot in the road. As her car goes careening out of control, she ignores (avoids acknowledging) her strong feelings of fear in order to cope effectively with the emergency at hand.

Disguise. Kirk is a smart student, whose parents are very proud of him. Both he and his parents have always expected that he will grow up to be a doctor and join his father's expanding medical practice, just as his older brother has. Until recently, Kirk has always done well in school. But now in his second semester of college, his grades have dropped sharply. Even though he *wants* to do well in school, and *wants* to please his parents, he finds himself paralyzed and test-anxious. After a horrible semester of guilt and struggle, he flunks two courses and has to leave school. The situation causes both Kirk and his parents great consternation.

What's going on with Kirk? Suppose he's motivated by a hidden rebelliousness against his parents' control over him. But he knows how important it is to his parents that he become a doctor, and he knows they only want the best for him. So he can't acknowledge his own rebelliousness, even to himself—he doesn't want to disappoint them and they certainly seem a lot more sure about his future than he feels himself. Instead, his longing for independence gets *disguised* as a lack of motivation and expressed in his neglect of his schoolwork.

In force terms, *disguise* is a mechanism whereby a force that cannot play itself out openly appears in masquerade. Kirk *looks* like an obedient child whose pre-med intentions have been thwarted by a puzzling motivational block, while he *actually* may be a young man who needs desperately to make his own decisions. The end result of the disguise is that Kirk's behavior proves quite thoroughly that only he and not his parents can determine his future—that is, this strong force is successfully played out, while looking like something else entirely.

Although Kirk's situation is certainly painful, disguise often has its adaptive benefits as does avoidance. A good example occurs when eleven-year-old Micky teases his classmate Bitsy in a friendly way. In his own pre-adolescent view of the world, Micky can't acknowledge that he likes her, so his affection is disguised as chiding. His teasing doesn't *look* like an expression of fondness for Bitsy, yet fondness is the hidden force.

103

Displacement. Ivy and her daughter, Liana, have a good relationship. They have worked out a lot of the logistical problems that inevitably arise between a working mother and a teenage daughter. Liana observes a strict curfew and contributes gasmoney for the occasional use of the family car, and Ivy trusts her to drive safely and behave responsibly. Every night this week, Ivy has given Liana permission to borrow the car to go study at her friend's house. Although this has caused Ivy some inconvenience, she knows how important it is for Liana to exercise her growing independence. But tonight, when Liana again asks for the use of the car, Ivy suddenly snaps, "*No*, you *can't* have the car tonight! I never get the car to myself any more!"

What's going on with Ivy? Suppose Ivy feels as though she is being taken advantage of at work, where she constantly has to do little errands or to work extra time. Because she is in a position of responsibility and her professional equanimity is extremely important, she can't openly acknowledge how overburdened she feels. Her resentment gets *displaced* onto Liana's request for use of the car.

In force terms, the mechanism of *displacement* operates when a force that cannot play itself out in its original context plays itself out in some other context. Since the force often seems to make less sense in its displaced context, we're less able to understand what's going on. We see that Ivy is angry, but she seems to be overreacting and we don't know what's really fueling her anger.

As with avoidance and disguise, displacement isn't always as problematic as it is in Ivy's situation. When George, for example, takes out his frustrations with his business partner on the raquetball court rather than on the job, he makes adaptive use of the mechanism of displacement. So long as he plays fair, his feelings of aggression and competition find an acceptable outlet rather than a maladaptive one.

In summary, forces can become hidden through several different mechanisms. Although these mechanisms contribute to our difficulty in identifying hidden forces, they all serve us well in some situations. Even when forces get hidden in ways that cause problems, we can understand it as an effort at adaptation. However misguided Ignatious's avoidance of his anger, the avoidance was designed to save him from Tamara's rejection. However disruptive Kirk's disguise of his rebelliousness, the disguise was designed to avert a rift between him and his parents. However unjustified Ivy's displacement onto her home life of her work-related resentments, the displacement was designed to preserve her high level of professional functioning. An important aspect of dealing with hidden forces, then, might be to find other more productive ways to meet these laudable goals.

The Annoying Ambiguity of Hidden Forces

Maureen chain smokes. After several serious efforts, she finds herself unable to quit. She claims that smoking calms her down, which, she says, she desperately needs. What's going on here?

Perhaps Maureen is simply the victim of the push-pull biochemical conditioning discussed in the previous chapter—no big mystery. But perhaps something deeper is going on. Consider that Maureen's mother, who succumbed several years ago to lung cancer, was also a heavy smoker. Maureen may feel a guilty compulsion to smoke too, because doing anything different would be like abandoning her mother. Or consider that Maureen also has an uneasy marriage with Winthrop. Among many points of tension, her husband disapproves of smoking—"It's unhealthy and unattractive." Maureen's persistent puffing may be disguised aggression directed at Winthrop.

All sorts of interpretations are possible! Hidden forces often are annoyingly ambiguous. As we warned in the previous chapter, we might even feel a temptation to "read in" hidden forces when a straightforward account will do. Indeed, if we put our minds to it, we can usually come up with *several* plausible hidden force explanations for any given situation. So how are we ever to know if there *is* a hidden force at work and *which* of several plausible possibilities really counts?

One way to address these questions is to give up the notion of hidden forces altogether. We could decide it's a lot easier just to take everything at face value, and to quit trying to read hidden meanings into everything. But we need to remember the reasons for positing hidden forces in the first place: When a person's conduct is hard to understand in terms of surface forces, hidden forces often help to explain it. Not wanting to surrender this source of insight, we simply have to cope with the problem of ambiguity.

Some Consequences of Ambiguity

So what are the ramifications of this ambiguity? What does it mean to our efforts to understand ourselves better? And what can be done to manage it?

One unpleasant consequence of ambiguity is the psychological pain of uncertainty—especially when the uncertainties concern our own basic nature. Imagine, for instance, that Maureen, through therapy, comes to recognize the three possible interpretations of her smoking sketched above. One can almost hear her inner dialogue: "Am I just a biochemical machine, then? Or my mother . . . am I that hung up on her? That's weird, but I guess those things happen. Or is it a fight with Winthrop? I didn't think I was a vindictive person but am I really, underneath? Maybe it's all these things . . . I can't tell who I am anymore!"

It's understandable that Maureen responds with confusion and alarm to her many hypotheses about herself. There is discomfort in the uncertainty of it all. In addition, Maureen finds herself reacting to her own reactions! She may be alarmed by her own confusion, horrified by her own possible motives, or perhaps relieved, even pleased with her courage in openly considering unpleasant possibilities. Whey people react not just to their situation but to some aspect of themselves—alarm at their confusion, fear of their anger, anger at their fears, etc.—they experience what we call a "second-order effect." As Maureen's anxiety suggests, second-order effects can be painful, sometimes even more painful than the circumstances that lead people to examine themselves in the first place. This very theme is the focus of a later chapter.

Besides the risk of uncertainty, the ambiguity of hidden forces presents us with the risk of being certain in the wrong way. On the one hand, people may reject too hastily hidden force accounts of their behavior. Suppose the therapist suggests to Maureen that her compulsive smoking is a way of getting back at Winthrop. "What nonsense," Maureen thinks. "That kind of psycho-babble messes people up. I know what I'm about: I like to smoke so much I can't give it up, and that's all there is to it." Of course, Maureen may be right. But she rejects out of hand a factor that might very well be involved. Indeed, one can imagine hidden force explanations of *why* she rejects it so adamently. Perhaps, not so straightforward as she claims, she fears her own messy psychological nature.

On the other hand, people often accept all too readily hidden force accounts that certainly call for careful critical scrutiny. Suppose the therapist proposes that Maureen is attacking Winthrop through her smoking. Maureen says, "Oh, I see. I never thought of that before. Sure, that must be what's going on. Oh my God! It all hangs together. I see deep down I must really hate Winthrop. Oh my God! And I never even knew it." Again, of course Maureen may be right. On the other hand, she takes as revealed truth a suggestion that certainly demands thoughtful assessment, and she rushes on to further hasty conclusions about the depth of her malice.

What to Do About Ambiguity

Seeking to identify hidden forces means risking the pain of uncertainty, of hasty acceptance, and of hasty rejection. But the fact is that significant parts of human behavior do not make sense without some sort of hidden force account. Trying to reduce ambiguity makes more sense than ignoring hidden forces.

What can we do, then? A solution neither perfect nor exciting, but at least easily said is: Be critical. It's important to remember that a hidden force account of a person's behavior is a theory, a hypothesis, an interpretation. As such, it needs to be tested critically against the reality of behavior. Does it really account for the behavior in detail? Does it provide a coherent picture not only of the particular behavior of most concern but other significant conducts as well? These are the sorts of questions that one asks of any good interpretation, and they must be asked of a

108

hidden force account—and indeed of a "surface" force account as well. It's not easy to be open and critical at the same time, but it's the best way to go.

Let's try it out by taking another look at Maureen and her smoking. We have two possible hidden force accounts on the table: She is hung up on her mother or out to get Winthrop. What questions might you ask to test whether either of these makes sense?

You could look for other ways besides smoking in which Maureen might play out the role of her mother. Or, remembering Edgar's subtle depression about his father's death, you could ask, "How does Maureen feel when the anniversary of her mother's death comes up?" "What memorabilia of her mother's does Maureen keep around and how does she feel about them?" The "mother" theory gets encouraged to the extent that you find a coherent pattern of additional information that supports that theory.

Now consider the "Winthrop" theory. You could ask, "Does Maureen smoke more when Winthrop is around than when he is not?" If she smokes to annoy him, she should smoke more when he is there. You could also look for other forms of passive aggression against Winthrop. Does she "forget" his birthday, for example, or consistently "misplace" things she borrows from him? Again, the "Winthrop" theory gets encouraged to the extent that a coherent pattern emerges.

Such probing is neither easy nor decisive. But coping with the inherent ambiguity of hidden force interpretations demands this sort of critical inquiry. One reason to seek professional psychological help is the complex art of critical inquiry needed, since it can be especially difficult to think clearly and critically when one is investigating one's own nature.

Beyond Ambiguity

With the question of ambiguity resolved as best we can, you'd hope that that would be the end of the problems with hidden forces. Not quite. Let's stand back, see where we are, and size up the next problem.

Our journey into the world of hidden forces can be summarized in a few sentences: Hidden forces give us a useful explanatory tool in making sense of initially puzzling behaviors. Forces can get hidden from our observation by accident or design. The mechanisms that hide forces are basically adaptive, intended to save us from the pain of overt conflicts or tensions. But they have a double edge—they often play a role in producing counterintentional behavior. Explaining our behavior in terms of forces is always an enterprise of making and testing theories, whether the forces are surface or hidden. But, by definition, when the forces are hidden, there's a lot more ambiguity involved in our efforts to make sense of our behavior. To earn the understanding made possible by considering hidden forces, we have to pay the price of coping thoughtfully and responsibly with the problems of ambiguity.

So suppose you succeed. You investigate, you ponder, and you arrive at a good theory about Maureen's problem, excluding rival theories. You tell Maureen about it (or perhaps you are Maureen), and let's say that Maureen ruminates awhile and believes you. Now Maureen and you have a fairly well developed insight into the nature of Maureen's problem.

Does it do any good?

In a way, the entire exploration of hidden forces so far has led up to this question. Sure, it's nice to understand what's going on down deep with some episode of counterintentional behavior. But does this insight help to change the behavior? The usual answer from the world of therapy has been, "Yes!" But in fact the question of whether, when and how insight helps is vexing enough to need a whole chapter of its own.

ThinkAbouts

What does all this mean to you? *How might you continue to think about the ideas presented in this chapter?*

• When you can see "no reason" for your behavior, remind yourself that there *are* forces at work—they're simply hidden from you for the moment. There are always reasons for your behavior, whether or not you are aware of them.

• Some forces are hidden "by accident," simply because you have overlooked them. Ask yourself, as a matter of routine, "Am I behaving as I intend? Why am I doing what I'm doing?"

• When there's no obvious explanation for your counterintentional behavior, the forces producing your behavior may be hidden "by design." They may be too painful or too embarrassing for you to acknowledge them comfortably. It takes some puzzling and courage to detect such hidden forces.

• Check some possibilities: Perhaps the forces causing your behavior aren't obvious to you because you are *avoiding* recognizing them at all. Perhaps the forces causing your behavior are hard to spot because they are *disguised* as other forces. Perhaps the forces causing your behavior aren't clear to you because they are *displaced* from another context.

• Revealing hidden forces is difficult and often painful, but it can leave you feeling that you know yourself a little better. Acknowledging who you really are—even if that means acknowledging

112

your pain—is often better than feeling mysteriously miserable and alienated from your own behavior.

• Speculating about hidden forces inevitably raises a lot of ambiguities. When faced with more than one possible interpretation, try not to accept or reject any of them too quickly. Rather, take the time to investigate them critically.

Chapter 4

SEEING THROUGH BLOCKS
Does Insight Help?

Cody is talking on the phone with his sister, Dodie. He tells Dodie about the big blow-up that happened at work today. It was already a pretty busy day, and then a colleague called Cody on the intercom and asked him for a copy of one of his old reports. The colleague was working on the firm's biggest project and needed Cody's old report for some crucial data. This sort of thing was common in the office, and Cody was always glad to be of help.

But Cody was really *very* busy, and every time this guy called to see if Cody had gotten hold of the old report yet, Cody still hadn't. The colleague was actually very patient, but Cody found himself getting angrier and angrier at this guy for hassling him. Finally, the colleague came by Cody's office to see if he could just pick up the report on the spot, and Cody ended up screaming at him. They actually had a shouting match in the hall outside Cody's office!

Cody is puzzled by his own behavior. It's not *like* him; there's no good *reason* for it. He hadn't intended to be so testy and uncooperative. He just didn't seem to be able to help himself. He wonders if he needs a vacation or something.

Then Dodie asks him, "Say, Cody, isn't this the same guy who beat you out for that big assignment last year? I remember you telling me that assignment should have been yours." "Oh . . . no, I mean, yes, this is the same guy. In fact, this is the same project! You know, I'd completely forgotten about that," Cody responds, a flood of bitterness washing through him. As they talk, it becomes clear to both of them that Cody harbors a lot of unacknowledged anger and resentment towards his colleague and that these feelings were influencing his behavior today.

At the end of the conversation, Cody says, "Well, that's a relief, in a way. Now I see why I was acting so strange. Dodie, thanks a lot."

In the last chapter we noted that hidden forces are a complicated business. Even when we deliberately go looking for hidden forces, they can be difficult to spot. So why do we bother? Why are we so motivated to seek insight?

We bother out of a sense that insight is important; that it matters *why* Cody was acting so uncharacteristically at work, for example. We want to know why we do what we do—you no doubt picked up this book because you wanted to better understand what counterintentional behavior is all about—but there's more to it than that. People don't usually want to understand their behavior *merely* for understanding's sake, just as you probably didn't buy this book out of idle curiosity.

Chances are good that in choosing this book you expected not simply to *understand* your behavior but, through understanding, to have greater *control* over it. When we feel helplessly incapable of doing what we intend and hopelessly puzzled by our incapacity, we expect insight to restore our control. In the midst of a counterintentional dilemma we find ourselves thinking, "Oh, if only I knew *why* I'm acting this way. . .!" We seek insight because we believe that insight is the key to solving our problems. Indeed, some deeply rooted traditions in psychotherapy believe the same thing.

Does insight really help us in the way we expect it to? Once we bring hidden forces to light, is our control restored? Does our block disappear? Is our problem solved?

Our own experience tells us that revealing the presence of a hidden force doesn't necessarily change anything at all. In the above scenario, for example, Cody realizes exactly *why* he was acting so testy at work, and yet this insight *may* or *may not* make any difference in how comfortable he is around his colleague *tomorrow*. After all, despite his insight, Cody is still angry; he's still harboring many unresolved feelings; and these feelings are still heightened in interactions with his co-worker. So Cody's insight into the hidden forces that caused him to blow up at work may not automatically give him any more control over his behavior than he had before.

Sometimes, insight can even make things worse. In the previous chapter, we speculated that forces get hidden by design as a mechanism for saving us from pain. In Cody's case, forgetting about his past rivalry with this particular colleague has helped him—until now—to maintain a civil and productive working relationship with him. But when Dodie brought the whole thing up again, Cody came face to face with his old feelings of anger and bitterness. Insight, then, threw a wrench in the works, making Cody more, not less uncomfortable—and possibly making it harder not easier for Cody to work with his colleague.

If insight doesn't always help, doesn't help automatically, and may even make things worse, what good is it? Why do we still look to insight as a solution to our problems? Perhaps we need to reexamine our assumptions about how insight helps.

The problem, really, is that our faith in the curative power of insight is almost magical. We simply expect that insight will help. When insight is indeed followed by improvement, we interpret it as proof of our expectations. Sure enough, insight solved the problem just as we knew it would.

But *how* did insight "solve" the problem? Problems don't simply vanish the moment they are exposed to the bright light of understanding. Insight helps, *when* it helps, in very specific ways. Let's take a look at three specific mechanisms whereby insight works.

Insight Improves Leverage

The better we understand the forces producing our behavior, the better our leverage in the situation. By leverage we mean increased means or opportunities for effecting our intentions.

It makes sense that we have better leverage with a more complete and accurate picture of our situation than we do with an incomplete or erroneous one. When we understand how and why things are working as they are, we can see more opportunities for control. We are in a position to wield our will to the best effect. Insight improves leverage by providing us with a better mental model of how things work, what causes what, and where we stand. In this way, insight allows us to see more alternative courses of actions and their effects, and helps us to better predict the effects of internal or external events upon us.

Example: Jordie agrees with his office mates that smoking is a "filthy habit." He knows it isn't good for his health; he doesn't even enjoy it much. He sees many reasons to stop and no reason why he shouldn't be able to. Since he thinks of himself as a straightforward and strong-willed sort of person, his only means to achieve his aim is "brute force"—simply changing his behavior by an act of will.

This approach may be successful, of course. But if it's not, there may well be hidden forces at work sustaining Jordie's counterintentional smoking behavior. If he sees "no reason" why he shouldn't be able to quit, and yet he just *can't* quit, then there must be some factors he *isn't* seeing.

How would insight help here?

Suppose Jordie realizes that he relies on smoking as a way to manage anxiety caused by his high-stress job and his perfectionism. When he smokes, he feels less anxious; when he doesn't, smoke, he feels more anxious. He is motivated to avoid anxiety so he ends up smoking despite his best intentions to quit.

This insight opens up a wide range of possible solutions that Jordie hadn't considered before. He could, for example, relieve his job stress by renegotiating his job description, hiring an assistant, or even finding another position. Or he could seek, through psychotherapy, to deal with the root causes of his perfectionism—perhaps it's a defense against deep feelings of unworthiness. Or he could simply find alternative ways to manage his anxiety, such as chewing gum, following an exercise regimen, or taking up meditation. Any one or a combination of these interventions may help Jordie quit smoking more effectively than his "brute force" approach. Insight has given Jordie leverage that he lacked without it.

Note that insight doesn't automatically solve Jordie's problem. And it alone doesn't solve the problem. Even when Jordie has come to recognize his smoking as an anxiety-management behavior, he still might not be able to think of any way to translate this knowledge into a reasonable course of action. Or, he may see all the interesting courses of action just described, but then fail to follow through on any of them. Just because Jordie has better insight into what's causing his smoking behavior doesn't mean that he automatically stops. It's what Jordie *does* with his insight—using it to guide his actions—that will make a difference.

Admittedly, insight may not help us when we are stuck in some truly uncontrollable situation. No amount of insight can help us accomplish an impossible end. Still, in these situations insight at least lets us know where we stand, and keeps us from uselessly beating our head against the wall. An old Irish prayer asks, "God grant me the strength to change the things I can, the courage to accept the things I can't, and the wisdom to know the difference." Insight can lend us wisdom of this sort, helping us understand the nature of our situation even if there's nothing we can do about it.

Insight Alleviates Second-Order Effects

When we find ourselves behaving counterintentionally, we often react with painful thoughts or feelings *about* ourselves. We call these self-referential thoughts or feelings "second-order" effects. For example: Not only are we smoking too much (a first-order effect), but we feel guilty for being so weak (a second-order effect); not only have we just binged on an ice cream soda (first-order effect), but we are angry at ourselves for having done it (second-order effect). A better understanding of *why* we are doing what we are doing can sometimes help us feel less guilty or angry. That is, insight can alleviate problematic *second*-order effects. (A more thorough discussion of second-order effects appears in Chapter 5.)

120

Example: Ever since she started college, Corkie has been having trouble with her coursework. She can't concentrate long enough to get her reading done, and she forgets the material as soon as she closes her book. After her first set of midterms, which are a disaster, Corkie resolves to work harder. "I did well in high school; there's no reason why I can't do well here." Corkie puts in more hours studying—many more than her roommates do—but to little effect; all she does is daydream. The harder she tries to work, the more guilty she feels about doing so poorly. She begins to think that there may be something wrong with her. She wonders if she is stupid, which depresses her, or if she has a learning disability, which scares her. She starts to think that maybe this was a big mistake and she's just not "college material."

How might insight alleviate Corkie's second-order distress?

Suppose after a long talk with her advisor, Corkie comes to realize how homesick she is. More insights follow: she realizes she has been feeling rather lost in such big lecture classes; she has had trouble pacing herself with the weekly and monthly assignments she has been getting in college compared to the daily assignments she got in high school; living away from home for the first time has been tougher than she thought it would be. No wonder she is having trouble concentrating! She can't help but dwell on thoughts of her family and her old friends, and of how much better things were last year when she was a senior in high school. She now understands that all this has been bothering her more than she gave it credit for.

Corkie's insight into her homesickness affects her second-order feelings in two ways. First, it serves to disconfirm some of her worse assumptions about what might be going on. Corkie can say to herself, "Oh, what a relief! I'm not crazy or stupid or lazy

121

at all—I'm preoccupied with adjusting to this new place." Second, her insights might make Corkie feel less lonely and less self-critical. She can say to herself, "Of course! It's understandable that I'd be having a hard time. Anybody in this same situation might feel and act this way."

Insight into the causes of her difficulties has relieved Corkie of some of her painful self-referential reactions. To the extent that these second-order effects exacerbated her difficulties in concentrating, Corkie may now find it easier to focus on her work despite her homesickness. Note, though, that such insight may not make her any less homesick than she was before. That is, the first-order force situation may not change much as a result of Corkie's insight, even if her insights do alleviate the second-order effects.

Insight Changes Forces by Changing Cognitions

The forces determining our behavior in a given situation are often grounded in cognition. That is, we are moved to *behave* in a particular way because of what we *think*. In certain circumstances, gaining insight can directly change a force at work by changing the underlying cognitions that give rise to the force.

In a way, the two mechanisms described above—insight improving leverage or alleviating second-order effects—are simply special cases of insight changing forces by changing our underlying cognitions. Since insight is essentially a cognitive event—insight itself is a kind of thinking—it *always* involves a change in our cognitions. Insight improves leverage or alleviates second-order effects precisely *because* we have come to conceive the situation differently. So why single out "changes in underlying cognitions" as a specific mechanism?

Notice that the two mechanisms discussed so far describe situations in which insight affects the forces only *indirectly*. When insight improves leverage, Jordie doesn't automatically stop smoking; rather, insight influences the judgments he makes about how he might best supply his will. And even when insight alleviates Corkie's second-order effects, her homesickness itself may not be affected; rather, insight changes how she feels or thinks about her behavior. In neither case does insight affect the forces at work directly.

In certain circumstances, however, insight brings about a change in a force directly and thus directly affects behavior. Suppose, for example, you are angry at your girlfriend because she is so late in arriving for your dinner date. You think she is being very inconsiderate; "she could have at least called." When she finally arrives you grumble angrily. Then, as she explains that the subway broke down and that she has been trapped for the past hour between stops, your anger evaporates—perhaps replaced with a hug.

What has happened here? The cognitive precondition for your initial anger is the thought that your girlfriend could have behaved differently than she did and that her lateness was the result of inconsiderateness. When your cognitions are corrected—when you learn that she was not responsible for her delay and was unable to call you—the angry emotions sustained by those cognitions disappear. You may still be disappointed that the dinner you cooked is now cold, or annoyed that the subways aren't kept in better working order, but you're no longer angry at your girlfriend for being inconsiderate.

In everyday situations like this, your initial anger gives rise to *pro*intentional behavior. That is, you experience your initial reaction to your girlfriend's lateness as a quite straightforward response to what seems to be a perfectly understandable situation. There's nothing strange about acting angrily when you think you have been mistreated. The key is that a change in your cognitions (a correction of your erroneous assumptions) resulted directly in a change in the forces at work. In *counter*-intentional situations, the mechanism is much the same. The forces producing your counterintentional behavior disappear when insight removes their cognitive underpinnings.

Example: Olive is about to take her first college midterm examinations, all five of which are scheduled for the same week. Although she realizes that this will be a stressful period for her, Olive feels generally confident and well-prepared since she has attended class regularly, done the assigned reading, and kept up with her homework. As her test week draws nearer, however, Olive becomes increasingly anxious. She can't stop thinking of the upcoming exams. She sleeps badly, insomnia interspersed with vague and uncomfortable dreams. The day of the first exam arrives, and as she is handed the test questions she is so nervous that she trembles. She tries to reassure herself that there's no reason to get upset, but she still has difficulty collecting her thoughts and the test goes very badly. Her second test the same afternoon goes even worse. Olive is of course very upset: it is clear to her that she isn't doing as well as she could given how thoroughly prepared she is. She is particularly frustrated because she is mystified by her own behavior. She decides to consult with a counselor before going to her next exam.

How might insight into her situation help?

Suppose it emerges, as she and her counselor discuss her

situation, that Olive has just recently made the difficult decision to "go pre-med." She has always loved science courses and done well in them (she chose to take three of them this semester), but her decision to major in biology and become a doctor is a very recent one. Her schoolwork has taken on a different meaning to her since she made the serious commitment.

The counselor points out to Olive that when she used to think of courses as fun and interesting and of tests as helpful evaluations of her work, she did quite well. But now Olive is treating these midterms as if her whole future depended on them. She has begun to think of her courses as nothing but pre-med requirements and her exams as obstacles to be overcome in the competition for a prized medical school spot. The counselor suggests that if this is what Olive is thinking, no wonder she is so anxious, and if she is so anxious, no wonder she isn't doing well. But, the counselor reminds her, her whole future does not in fact depend on the outcome of her first midterms freshman year. They are not the sole determinant of her potential as a doctor. They are only one set of a great many such exams she will take in her academic lifetime, and thinking of them in other terms has only robbed her of her enjoyment in learning.

As Olive gains insight from these formulations, she finds that her feelings about her remaining exams become considerably less distressed. As the counselor's comments revise her cognitive perspective, the forces sustaining her test anxiety dissipate. As she ceases to think of her current midterms as a one-chance shot at her entire future, she finds herself less anxious about them, so she feels capable of a better performance. Olive may well remain anxious about her commitment to medical training, of course, and she and the counselor may decide to continue conversations around this subject. However, her counterintentional test behavior will abate as the forces that produce it lose their cognitive underpinnings.

Insight tends to work in this direct way when the problematic behavior is caused primarily by a single force which in turn is based primarily on a single cognition. Many situations, of course, don't fit this double bill. On the one hand, it often happens that more than one strong force participates in producing a behavior. For example, Olive's test anxiety and poor performance may be caused not only by her attitude towards the exams, but also by an unrecognized deficit in college-level study skills. She can't solve her chemistry problems, which makes her anxious, which makes it even harder for her to concentrate, which makes her even more anxious, and so on. Not just her cognitions, but her poor study skills contribute to the problem. On the other hand, it often happens that a force results from several contributing factors. Remember when your girlfriend got stuck in the subway and was late for dinner. Suppose your anger at your girlfriend's inconsiderateness arises not only from her tardiness on this particular night but also from your long frustrating experience with her irresponsible behavior. So you feel not only vivid anger because you think she has been inconsiderate, but also old harbored anger from past incidents, anxiety about whether your girlfriend really cares for you, and fear for the future of the relationship. Your anger is based not on a single perception but on a number of contributing thoughts.

When such complexities exist, insight doesn't directly and immediately affect the forces at work, and so we tend to feel that insight has "failed": Olive has seen her exams for what they are and yet continues to be anxious and to do poorly; you have learned of your girlfriend's subway delay and yet you still feel angry and hurt. When insight "fails," it is worth asking *why* and *how* it might have "failed." What *other* forces might be at work besides those revealed through the insight? What *other* bases may there be for the forces at work besides cognitive ones.

Insight as an Ongoing Process

Jordie, Corkie and Olive were each helped by insight in specific ways. We don't mean to imply that these are the only ways in which insight can help, of course. Psychoanalytic theory, for example, suggests that emotional insight makes it possible for an individual to "work through" his heretofore unconscious impulses and conflicts. So our three models of how insight helps are hardly exhaustive.

Even in our three straightforward cases, we see that insight isn't necessarily enough: Jordie might take no action despite his many options, Corkie could remain horribly homesick despite her self-understanding, and Olive might find that her renewed perspective only highlights the counterintentionality of her behavior. It is particularly painful to have insight without control; to know why you are doing something counterintentional and yet still feel helpless to do otherwise. At moments like these we feel miserably disappointed in our hopes for that magical cure.

If insight can't be counted on to solve our problems, is it worth the effort? The answer is, "Sure." There's no point in dismissing a resource like insight just because it isn't the cure-all we often expect it to be. We have argued above that we should simply replace our notion of insight-as-a-cure-all with some more specific models of how insight helps when it helps. Insight helps by improving leverage, reducing second-order effects, or changing the cognitions that sustain a force.

127

Models like these help us think more critically about our behavior by giving us specific questions to ask ourselves. Suppose Cody, for example, in our opening scenario, finds that his insight into the reasons for his problematic behavior helps him to feel more comfortable around his colleague. He might want to ask himself, "Why? How exactly did insight make a difference? Has my new understanding improved my leverage? Has insight relieved painful second-order effects? Has it changed the cognitive basis for my behavior?" He may even find that insight has helped him in more than one of these ways. And what if Cody's insights *don't* make a difference to how comfortable he is around his colleague? Well, then, he can ask "Why not? Are there other forces at work that I have overlooked? Or are there reasons for my behavior that aren't cognition-based?"

These questions, you'll notice, are questions asked in retrospect, after-the-act, so to speak. But once you are aware of the ways in which insight helps, you can ask questions of yourself before-the-act, as well. You needn't wait around for insight to "strike." For example, you might actively *seek* insight into your counterintentional behavior in an effort to improve your leverage in the situation. Or you can actively question what cognitions underlie your motives or emotions, in order to examine and possibly revise them.

You're probably thinking, "But at this rate I'd constantly be asking myself *why* all the time!" Exactly so. This doesn't mean that one has to be compulsively reflective, or spend life gazing at one's navel. But frequent reflection can help enormously in understanding one's circumstances and options. A good personal philosophy about reflection and insight might run something like this:

Insight can best help when we treat it as an ongoing process, not just a finished product. Any analysis of the forces influencing a person's behavior at a given moment, however insightful, is a constructed meaning. It is a model we have built to try to capture something of our experience and hold it before us so that we can look at it and come to understand it. But the *subject* of our model-building is not static; life goes on; the "circle of causation" is in constant motion; the force field is always in flux. Even the process of inquiry itself introduces changes in the force situation. Furthermore, an analysis of any one behavior is necessarily a drastic simplification of a bigger picture. When we seek insight, then, we need to recognize the value of simple and static models while at the same time recognizing the complex and dynamic nature of life and experience. And this demands that we direct our efforts not towards producing a final explanation but towards engaging in an ongoing process of "meaning making"—asking ourselves "Why?" not just once, but on a regular basis.

Hidden Forces, Insight, and the Self

So yes, insight into the hidden forces producing our behavior can relieve our sense of helplessness and help us behave as we best intend. Insight doesn't help as automatically, magically or reliably as we might wish. Rather, insight helps, when it helps, in specific ways. Most importantly, making good use of insight involves not just accumulating stock answers or looking for certainties, but rather engaging in an evolving process of continual speculation.

Where has all this led us? Clearly, the notion of hidden forces discussed in the last chapter is a powerful tool in our efforts to make sense of our behavior. Moreover, an understanding of how insight works can help us take better control of our behavior. At the same time, a whole new range of questions emerges. If forces can be hidden from us, and we can gain insight into our own behavior, and we can have thoughts and feelings *about* our thoughts and feelings (second-order effects), then where is our true "self?" It is as though there must be more than one "self" within us—otherwise, how could forces *within* ourselves be hidden *from* ourselves? Similarly, when we gain insight into ourselves, who is looking at whom? Which are our true thoughts and feelings, those of the first or those of the second order? These puzzling questions are addressed in the following chapter.

ThinkAbouts

*What does all this mean to you? How might you continue
to think about the ideas presented in this chapter?*

• Sometimes, insight into *why* you are behaving in counterintentional ways helps you gain more control of yourself. Insight doesn't *always* help—it's not a magical cure—but it helps in some specific ways.

• Insight can help by improving your leverage in a situation. When you feel you have some insight into the forces producing your behavior, try translating this information into a course of action. What leverage does your knowledge provide? What intervention points does it suggest?

• Insight can help by making you feel better about yourself and your situation. When you feel you have some insight into the forces producing your behavior, you may be able to be more compassionate towards yourself. Try to see your behavior as "understandable-given-the-circumstances," rather than "senseless," "weak" or "stupid."

• Insight can help by challenging the cognitive rationale underlying your behavior. If you can identify and examine your unspoken *reasons* for behaving as you are, you will often find that they are not so sound as you assumed. Once your reasoning changes, your behavior can, too.

• We often think of insight as a completed thought or analysis. "Well, that's that!" we're likely to say, "Now I have insight." But perhaps insight is better understood as a *process*, an ongoing, adaptive, constructive effort to understand. So keep at it!

131

Chapter 5

BLOCK UPON BLOCK

Fear of Fear and Other Force Spirals

Winston and Kent have been best friends since elementary school. Winston enjoys Kent's company and recognizes that their friendship is based on long-standing affection and respect. He likes Kent's sense of humor, knows he can say whatever's on his mind, and feels secure in their relationship.

Winston gets a call from Kent, who invites him out for a pizza that night. "After dinner," says Kent, "maybe we could meet up with my new friends and check out a big dance party." "Sure," Winston answers readily.

They joke all through dinner. But after their pizza, when he and Kent meet up with Kent's friends, a change comes over Winston. He finds himself suddenly quiet and tense, even tongue-tied—almost a different person from the easygoing and funny guy he was at dinner. Now, every time he thinks of something to say, he immediately wonders. "Will I say something stupid?" When he misses one chance after another to chime in, he feels like kicking himself. His anger with himself makes it even more difficult for him to follow the flow of conversation, and when there is a pause, he just feels blank.

133

Worst of all, Winston fully realizes how differently he is acting than he was at dinner. He wishes he could just be himself, but the harder he tries the more self-conscious he gets. Finally, as the group heads off to the party, Winston excuses himself and just goes home. He leaves feeling angry and unlikeable, wondering, "Why am I so pathetic?"

What happened here? Winston was enjoying himself in the company of his friend, with no counterintentional behavior in sight. But, with the larger group of Kent's friends, suddenly Winston's experience became quite different. He watched himself behave in a way he didn't like and felt no control over.

Looking at basic force concepts may help us understand Winston's transformation. At first, with only Kent for company, all the forces favored Winston's easy sociability: for example, Winston's trust in Kent's respect for him, his confidence that Kent would laugh at his jokes, and his enjoyment of Kent's company. But Kent's new friends brought in some new force: perhaps Winston was jealous of them or feared their rejection. This new force produced Winston's social discomfort and uncharacteristic silence.

We'll call this way of understanding the situation a "first-order" analysis. It deals with "first-order" forces, by which we mean forces arising from Winston's encounter with his environment. Winston's tongue-tied counterintentional behavior certainly makes sense in terms of first-order forces.

Still, something seems to be left out of the picture. The first-order forces don't include Winston's painful *self*-consciousness. Not only did Winston encounter the world, he also encountered himself. Not only did he have thoughts and feelings and responses to his external environment, but he also had thoughts and feelings and responses to his own thoughts and feelings and responses.

It's not hard to empathize with this side of Winston's experience. We all have some consciousness of our selves and we all experience moments when that self-consciousness is painful. We can imagine Winston's internal voice: "I should say something now . . . Boy, do I feel like a jerk. I can tell I'm coming across like a really dull guy. Why aren't I saying something? I wonder if my nervousness shows. I just hate myself." For Winston, this self-consciousness, or encounter with himself, itself gave rise to forces that influenced his behavior.

Let's call the forces that arise from encounters with yourself "second-order" forces. Such forces represent the self-consciousness that gets left out of the first-order analyses. And second-order forces often seem to contribute as much or more to counterintentional behavior as first-order forces! Sure, Winston first became tense in response to his environment—those new friends of Kent's. But then he became alarmed at his own tension, and then angry at his own silence. Maybe his first-order jealousy or fear of rejection wouldn't have been enough to make him so tongue tied. But the second-order forces did him in.

Remember the old tale about the centipede. A spider observes a centipede walking by, and says "I can't tell you how much I admire the way you walk. I can hardly manage my own six legs; how can you possibly manage with a hundred legs at once?" Whereupon the centipede, who had simply been walking along without a thought about it, suddenly becomes so aware of her many legs that she collapses in a tangle. Second-order effects do seem to gum up the works like this, making things more complicated. They confuse our efforts to understand and to control our behavior. If we encounter not just the world but also our selves, and if we have thoughts and feelings and reactions to our own thoughts and feelings and reactions, and if these affect our ultimate behavior, how can we ever sort things out?

In the next section, we lay out a better map of the problem by expanding our earlier notion of a circle of causation into a sort of spiral of causation. Then we look into why such second-order reactions occur at all: are they really just troublemakers? On the contrary, we'll argue that second-order effects usually do a lot of good and only sometimes go wrong. Then the question comes up: do we ever experience "third-order effects"—thinking about thinking about thinking? And if this happens, do we risk becoming infinitely removed from the "real world" in an ever-ascending spiral of self-observation?

The fact that we can observe and react to ourselves also raises this real puzzler: What is the "self?" Is it located in the observer or in the observed? How is it that you can observe some side of yourself as though it were not part of yourself? How can you feel alienated from your own behavior or mystified by your own motives? After all, they're *yours!* How do you draw the line between the Self and the Not-Self? We'll tackle these puzzling questions and then end the chapter on a more concrete note, considering how second-order effects most commonly contribute to counterintentional behavior and how to manage them better.

A Spiral of Causation

We have nothing to fear but fear itself. *
—Franklin Delano Roosevelt

We talk easily of people fearing their own shame, or love, or even fearing their own fear. Or people may become ashamed of their fear, their love, or even ashamed of their shame. Not only angry at others, we may become angry with ourselves, and even angrier at ourselves for being angry with ourselves. We all

136

recognize these compound reactions. But just acknowledging their reality doesn't help us to talk about them clearly.

One key to clear talk is to recognize that in all these compound reactions people are reacting to themselves—to their own perceptions, the forces evoked, the reactions they display, and so on. If Norris is afraid of gorillas, gorillas are the object of his fear. Now what if Norris is afraid of himself in some way—say, his tendency to lose his temper or to gamble to excess? That makes his fear a second-order effect. Second-order effects aren't always a bad thing; they can have a positive as well as a negative tone. If Amy has confidence in her own abilities, the object of her confidence is something about herself, so her confidence is a second-order effect.

To get a better picture of all this, we can diagram a circle of causation for second-order effects, just as we did earlier with with first-order effects. In fact, let's add the "second-order" circle to the diagram presented earlier (see figure on next page) to make plain how effects can "spiral" from the first circle to the second circle.

You can see that the second circle resembles the first completely, except for one key point: the "input" to the second circle comes from our encounter with the first circle, rather than from our encounter with the world out there.

To understand how all this works, let's consider an episode as it loops its way around both circles. Niles, seventy-one and retired for several years, lives with his daughter and her husband and family. Niles wants to contribute to his grandchildren's upbringing but doesn't want to be intrusive—a delicate balance. Niles encounters Sue, his twelve-year-old granddaughter, heading out into the snowy winter with only a light jacket on. "Say there," Niles says, "shouldn't you dress a little more warmly?"

"Oh, Gramps," says Sue. "Don't baby me," and with a toss

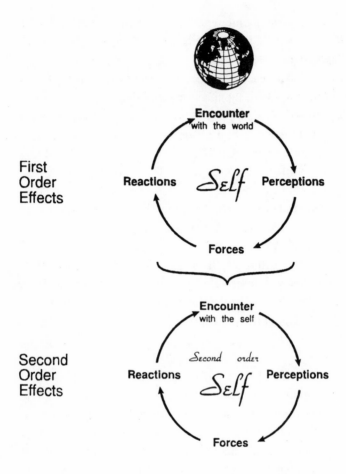

First
Order
Effects

Second
Order
Effects

The Second Order Circle of Causation

of her head, she's out the door. Niles frowns to himself, thinking that once again he has butted in where he didn't belong. "I won't get involved next time," he vows to himself.

The first-order circle here is plain enough. Niles encounters and perceives the environment: his granddaughter leaving with too light a jacket. A force—concern—is evoked, leading to his reaction—encouraging her to dress more warmly. This in turn generates a new encounter with the world—Sue responds with her "Oh, Gramps."

Now things get a little more complicated. A response "spirals up" to the second circle. The "Oh, Gramps" prompts Niles to encounter himself, not just the environment. Niles perceives himself as having once again intruded by caring too much, or at least too openly. This perception brings up forces that make Niles angry with himself, and he reacts, resolving to be more careful in the future. If he follows through, that would change both how he behaves later (first circle) and the self he encounters later (second circle).

Notice that Niles might not have experienced any second-order effects at all. Another natural reaction to Sue's "Oh Gramps" would have been anger at *Sue* rather than at *himself*. He might have simply muttered, "Ingrate! The new generation just has no manners at all!" Or he might have insisted that Sue change her coat. Such reactions would involve another turn around the *first-order* circle of causation, but no spiraling up to the second order.

Adaptation and Overshoot

What are we to make of this complicated double looping? Why is it there at all?

Actually, as we mentioned above, the main function of the second-order circle is quite positive. The second circle brings the ability to reflect on yourself—and so to change yourself. With the first circle alone, we can deal with our circumstances solely by acting on the environment. With the second circle in place, we can also act on ourselves. Niles, for example, can reflect on himself and his behavior and consider how to act in the future. The second-order circle brings with it not only self-consciousness, but also self-perception and possibilities for self-control.

Examples of such payoffs are everywhere. Fear may cloud Martha's judgment, but, knowing this, she can try to reassure herself. A drinking habit may get Arnold into trouble, but recognizing the pattern is his first step toward changing it. Trying to learn a new dance step may frustrate Rhoda, but she recognizes the frustration as something that usually happens when she learns something new, so she doesn't let it stop her. In general, *knowing oneself* creates an opportunity to *have more control over oneself.*

Despite the generally adaptive nature of second-order effects, there are limits to the power the second-order circle brings us. We often find it hard to quell fear or anger; habits may prove stubborn; we may give in to frustration. When we try to take hold of ourselves, our selves may prove slippery. This is a little disappointing, though not surprising. Situations in the external environment—bridge building, child rearing, job hunting—are hard to handle for all sorts of reasons; similarly, managing the self is no picnic.

In fact, the second circle occasionally can make problems worse, as we saw in Winston's case. Second-order effects can be problematic in two ways. For one thing, second-order effects, like first-order effects, may be too extreme. Consider George,

140

who is a little overweight but not obese. George finds it hard to reduce—he is blocked there. But that in itself might be manageable. Agonizing over his own weakness and feeling ugly are what cause him the most pain. George's biggest problem is not that he is blocked from losing weight but that he feels such intense shame about himself.

Or consider Millicent, who constantly nags herself for being a softy while she continues to give and give. People can of course give too much—to the point of self-destruction. But maybe Millicent is just a rather giving person who would like to be a little less giving and finds it hard to change the pattern. Millicent's biggest problem may not be that she is too giving, but rather that she has built up this image of herself as a soft touch and compulsively nags herself about it. George's weight and Millicent's generosity are small first-order problems, but George's shame and Millicent's self-criticism are big second-order problems.

Another way in which the second circle can cause problems is by contributing to a spiraling escalation of an initially first-order difficulty. For example, George, like many overweight individuals, may eat to escape from worry. The world can't bother him when it is obscured by a sandwich. Now the following spiral sets in: George is a bit overweight and has trouble reducing—a first-order difficulty. George becomes ashamed of his "weakness"— a second-order effect. Feeling bad, George feels all the more inclined to eat because the snack helps him to forget his worries for a while. So George gets even chubbier, feels even more ashamed, gets even hungrier, and so on.

And how about Millicent? She begins to feel that she is *too* kind—too easily taken advantage of. So she nags herself to be tougher, feeling at the same time guilty about having grudging thoughts. To compensate for the guilt, Millicent becomes even more giving, only to see herself as even more of a patsy, and so on.

In summary, the second circle has the mixed characteristics of all the mechanisms talked about in this book. Like forces, weak additivity, and so on, the second circle fundamentally works for us. At the same time, sometimes it overshoots, generating problems that otherwise would not be there. That is, second-order effects serve basically positive and adaptive functions, which only sometimes go awry.

Third-Order Thinking

Wheels within wheels, circles upon circles—how far can we go with this? How far is it useful to go? Well, consider the plight of chubby George one more time. Remember that George, not so very overweight, nonetheless feels anxious about his weight and snacks to escape from his anxiety. Now suppose George takes a long hard look at what he is doing. "This is ridiculous," George says to himself. "I'm just digging myself deeper into a hole. I'm going to cut that out." Every time George feels an impulse to snack, he cross-checks himself. "Am I really hungry or am I just anxious? Since I had lunch an hour ago, I'm probably just anxious. I'll take a walk instead of a snack."

The same kind of story also could be told about Millicent, who might end up catching herself with such words as, "Am I just acting super nice so I won't feel guilty later? Yeah, I guess so. Well, reasonably nice is good enough."

What do you call it when George becomes aware of his second-order snacking circle? You might say that this is a "third-order effect.'' At the second order, George looks at his fatness and reacts to that. At the third order, George looks at his thinking *about* his fatness and reacts to *that*. ''Standing above'' his own thinking about himself gives George insight into how he behaves and leverage over it.

With such third-order reflective thinking in mind, our diagram can be updated to display three circles, as on the next page.

In other words, in third-order effects, you encounter yourself engaging in self-encounters. As discussed earlier, second-order effects can be vicious circles. In some third-order thinking, you ''stand above'' such a vicious circle, see it for what it is, and, with luck and wit, get the leverage to break it. In other moments, you can simply contemplate second-order circles with interest without trying to alter them. You might even encourage yourself to continue a second-order circle, if it's a useful, rather than problematic, one.

The key move here is stepping back from what you couldn't see clearly before—making an object of it. In second-order effects, you make an object of yourself, seeing your own bad eating habits, quick temper or selfless giving. This may give you insight into and power over your behavior. By making an object of the second-order circle itself, you gain insight into your own self-referential thinking and gain power over that.

This exercise of pulling back from your situation and making it an object could get out of hand. No doubt third-order thinking sometimes leads to vicious circles. Should we then look to fourth-order thinking to correct glitches in the third order, fifth-order to correct glitches in the fourth, and so on? Where will it all end?

But no need to go overboard. It's important to remember that we're looking for useful ways to talk about the play of forces in

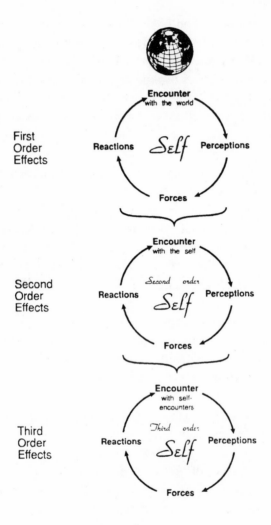

First
Order
Effects

Second
Order
Effects

Third
Order
Effects

The Third Order Circle of Causation

people. The three orders do this job well enough in most situations. It doesn't seem especially interesting or useful to talk about orders beyond the third, so we rarely do. But there is an important reason to go *as far* as the third: It is through third-order thinking that we recognize and often remedy how we compound our own difficulties with second-order reactions.

The Constructed Self

When Lorraine reads her phone bill, her eyes open wide. "Did *I* make all those calls?!" she wonders, collapsing back into the couch. "How could I have *done* that?" She had promised herself—she had *sworn* to herself—that she'd cut back her long-distance calls, yet here is a whopping big bill. She replays the previous month like a movie: she watches as her excited self dialed to tell mom about the head chef's praise, and then, that next week, as the same self called friends on the other coast to shriek about the promotion—four friends for an hour apiece!—and then she watches the spellbound self picking up the phone day after day for three weeks, for those flirty chats with Duane in Connecticut. She didn't intend to call so much, but she just didn't think about that when she actually picked up the phone. "Well," she mutters now, "this month, I'm not gonna let myself get carried away."

So who is the real Lorraine? Is it the impulsive Lorraine who gets carried away day by day and makes those calls? Is it the dispassionate Lorraine who stands back and reviews her telephoning behavior objectively? Is it the well-meaning Lorraine who swears to take herself in hand?

For us, standing apart from Lorraine's dilemma, the answer is easy: those are *all* the real Lorraine. But for Lorraine, "who she

145

really is'' doesn't get resolved so neatly. In her eyes, she isn't *really* the impulsive one who makes those calls. She's *really* the orderly in-control one who's now going to take herself in hand. In other words, Lorraine counts some aspects of her behavior as ''really'' hers and seems to count others as ''not really'' hers.

Does it matter how Lorraine partitions up what's really her and what isn't? You bet. Because Lorraine's map of her true Self is likely to influence how successfully she deals with her counter-intentional behavior.

For example, if she *doesn't* recognize her telephoning as ''really hers''—saying, ''Oops, I goofed! That wasn't *me*! I'll do better next month!''—she may underestimate how hard it's going to be to take herself in hand. The result will be that she doesn't devise a strong enough plan to change her behavior. If she *does* admit, ''That was *me*! I really blew it! I'm a phonaholic!'' she might be in a better position to deal seriously with her thoughtless dialing impulses—perhaps with a strategic application of the will. (She might decide to move all the chairs away from the telephone, for example, making it uncomfortable to talk for long.) Alternatively, she may decide, ''Those calls are important to *me*. *I* really want to make 'em,'' and, unless Lorraine is in a real financial bind, a good resolution for her might be to go ahead and make the calls and quit castigating herself about it. She can simply decide to deliberately forego some other expense in order to afford her phone bills.

So, yes, it matters what Lorraine sees as her true Self, and she can construe her true Self in more than one conceivable way.

Which Is the Real You?

The Bureau of Standards in Washington settles questions of measurement—what really counts as a foot or a pound, and so

146

on. But as to "what's really us," there is no bureau in Washington dictating a neat policy. The rules for what is Self and what is Not-Self seem rather changeable, as we saw with Lorraine. Even our most basic assumptions about the nature of the Self don't hold up to scrutiny. Let's explore this a bit.

Most people, if asked to define the boundaries of their real Self, feel that at least they can identify their Self as what's inside their skin. Most minimally and undeniably, your physical body is clearly your Self, right? Well, more or less. Do you consider your duodenum part of yourself? Sure, but you probably don't think about it much. What about a splinter in your thumb? Certainly not, even though it *is* inside your skin. What about a cancer in your body? Hard to say; it's both Self and Not-Self depending on how you look at it. What about a fetus in your womb? Hard to say, again. You see, things get complicated.

And what about some things outside your skin? Are those so clearly *not* part of your Self? You can imagine someone saying, quite sincerely, "I've had that teddy bear up in the closet since I was a kid. I only look at it maybe once a year. But, you know, losing it would be like losing part of myself!" For other people, their collection of '50s rock singles or their Alfa Romero may be a strongly felt part of themselves. And many people think of loved ones—spouse, children, parents—as parts of themselves. Of course, yet other people throw away their teddy bears and rock singles without a qualm when cleaning the attic, think of their cars as "just transportation," and may not even be all that attached to their immediate families.

No, indeed, there's no bureau in Washington, and seemingly no clear standards at all defining what is one's Self. We can't even clearly define the boundaries of the physical Self, never mind the psychological Self! But if there's no one answer to "What's the real Self," how do people end up with notions of who they are? After all, we *are* who we are, and seem to feel pretty intact most of the time. If there are no strict rules, how is it that our individual Selves nevertheless carry on quite well?

The Geography Analogy

Broadly speaking, people "construct" images of themselves over time. How this process works—how the boundaries of the Self get constructed—can be described by way of analogy with another context in which boundaries are defined. Think of the boundaries of states and nations.

The position of a national boundary reflects a complex negotiation of governments with one another and with circumstance. Of course, a river or a mountain range may provide a natural guideline. But, if they value the river or mountain range, each nation will want it. Where battles are won and lost, where trade flows strong or trickles, or simply where a line is drawn arbitrarily just to settle the matter neatly—all are factors that may shape national boundaries.

Just as rivers and mountain ranges provide natural boundary markers for nations, your skin does the same thing for the Self. But just as political or economic interests can override those boundary markers for nations, so psychological and emotional interests can override these boundary markers for the Self. Just as wars, elections, and negotiations can change the boundaries of nations, so with the Self: new experiences and new assessments of importance and convenience can lead us to remake our old maps.

But can we *arbitrarily* make up who we "really" are? Well, no. Neither, after all, can nations make up their boundaries any

148

old way they please. Cultural cohesions and the natural geography exert a considerable influence. Likewise with our human Selves, the natural geography of the skin and the social geography provided by various cultural customs influence our boundary-making. Even so, we still find quite a lot of room for negotiation. So the Self, in considerable part, is defined by how we construe ourselves rather than by some strict criterion.

Do we *deliberately* go about making up who we are? Well, not usually. We just feel ourselves to *be* ourselves most of the time. The borders shift gradually over the years, or abruptly when circumstances lead us to reconsider who we are. Even then, we typically don't realize that we're actively rearranging the borders. Usually we fix our attention on the immediate crisis—how can I make sense of this, what can I do, how can I come to terms—and may not even notice the broader changes such episodes can cause.

To return to the geography metaphor again, the boundaries of the Self are established not through one or a few calculated acts but more through a complicated and somewhat haphazard history. This notion of the constructed Self makes a lot more common sense, when you think about it, than a rigid notion. It also has important implications for the problem of counterintentional behavior and ways to combat that problem. In particular, people often may be unnecessarily trapped by the way they construe the Self, where they draw their boundaries. Remember that, because of second-order effects, how we see ourselves has a great influence on how we feel and behave. Perhaps, then, by seeing ourselves in new ways, by *re*constructing our visions of ourselves, we can undo old boundaries and free ourselves from second-order problems.

Ownership

Imagine three soap opera fans in their sixties. Grace, Fred and Wilma. Grace is an enthusiast. At this stage of her life, she views her heartfelt involvement in the soaps as the brightest thing in her day, the spark that keeps her going. "Oh, they exaggerate so," she acknowledges. But she welcomes them enthusiastically, unperturbed by such criticism. If asked, she would place her enthusiasm for soaps inside the border of her essential Self. You might say she "owns" her involvement with the soaps.

Fred, on the other hand, is a reluctant fan. He feels rather stupid sitting down every day in front of "the boob tube." He is drawn and repelled at the same time. While watching faithfully, he constantly carps about the ridiculous plots. From time to time, he criticizes himself as well: "Why do I sit here watching this nonsense; I don't know why I bother." Fred places his attraction to soaps emphatically outside the boundary of his Self. One might say that he "disowns" his attraction to the soaps, viewing it as an unfortunate weakness of a Self that is essentially too lofty for such stuff.

Wilma contrasts with both. She watches just as often as Fred and Grace, but without thinking much about it one way or another. She neither reproaches herself nor delights in watching. It's just something she does for fun and to pass the time; it's not important one way or another. Wilma does not place her soap watching inside or outside the borders of her true Self. One might say that for Wilma watching the soaps is an "unowned" behavior.

The stories of Grace, Fred and Wilma make plain the general sense of "owned," "disowned" and "unowned." The three concepts offer broad ways of classifying a person's attitude toward some feeling, force, behavior or whatever, that might be taken as part of the Self or not. When you "own" some characteristic, you view it as inside the border, part of your essential and fundamental Self. When you "disown" such a characteristic, you treat it as alien, invasive, unwelcome, not really you. When you "unown" such a characteristic, your posture is more one of unreflective indifference; the characteristic simply lacks sufficient importance to place one way or the other in relation to the Self.

As emphasized earlier, the boundaries of the Self are flexible. For Fred, the "disowned" characteristic causes trouble and, in particular, counterintentional behavior. But if the ownership gets changed—the boundaries of the Self reconstructed in a new image—the difficulties may lessen or vanish. Four examples follow.

From disowning to owning: The benefits of acceptance. Dodge never could understand children, although he didn't mind having them around. He and his wife raised two and got along just fine. But his wife had a much deeper relationship with them, while Dodge seemed to care about them from a distance. Now that both children are grown and off on their own, things are still about the same. Dodge is on straightforward and comfortable terms with them—not close, like his wife, but comfortable.

The problem is that Dodge keeps wondering lately if there's something wrong with him as a father. Fathers on TV, for example, seem much more demonstrative and openly affectionate with their kids, while that's never really been Dodge's style. He knows that he—his real Self—loves his kids, but he wonders if maybe there's a cold streak in him or something, that has prevented him from showing it in the ways he thinks he's supposed to.

Perhaps Dodge could learn to be more involved and expressive with his kids. But, as a minimum goal, perhaps he just needs to learn to be comfortable with himself. He is suffering from the second-order effect of disliking something he identifies as alien in himself, something he disowns as a "cold streak." He might learn to think of himself in a different way: "Okay, so I'm not a lovey-dovey kind of guy. Big deal. I provided well, I love my kids, I'm on good terms with them, they've grown up to be responsible folks raising their own families. Let me take myself as I am and stop moping about it." In fact, if Dodge could fully own, rather than disown, his naturally rather formal interpersonal style, he might paradoxically find it easier to loosen up a little.

From disowning to owning, another example: The benefits of responsibility. May Lou swats her kids. She doesn't intend to, of course. She says so herself: "I don't mean to. I love 'em both. Something just comes over me. It builds up, and whap!"

May Lou may be disowning her violent reactions as a way of refusing to face up to them. Disowning in general can be a strategy for evading responsibility for your own actions. May Lou might find herself better able to control her violence if she received help in thinking about her behavior according to a different pattern: "That's *me* swatting my kids, not anyone else. It's *me* that does it. It's *me* that lets myself do it. Okay, I love them, but obviously I feel frustrated and angry and desperate, too, and I have to find better ways of dealing with my situation than hitting the kids." May Lou can't help how she feels, but owning her feelings may be a first step towards changing her behavior.

From owning to disowning: The benefits of "reaction against control." Maurice is a compulsive gambler. "I love it," he admits. "It's when I'm most alive. Oh, I know I'm making a mess of my life—I mean, I do want to keep my job and keep my family fed. But when I'm at the track, I'm so alive, nothing else matters! I love it!"

Maurice owns and glories in his compulsion, at the same time that he knows it is destructive. Maurice might do better if he *dis*owned his gambling: "I have this thing in me that wants to gamble. This thing is no real friend of mine. It gives me a high but meanwhile it's really ruining me. It's like a parasite, living off my life until there's none of me left. It's a disease."

Disowning a problematic feeling or impulse often triggers a very general human reaction that might be called "reaction against control." People hate to be controlled, as a rule, and often fight back with stubborn persistence. Disowning a characteristic can cast it in the role of "other," and hence invoke a reaction against control—against the "other."

From owning to unowning: Shedding shame. Rocky, a disturbed teenager, is privately obsessed with a one-inch strawberry birthmark on his left cheek. It is not really very large, but it looms large in his eyes. He writes in his diary: "You know, this thing on my face is me. Sometimes I wake up at night and it's like I imagine it glowing in the dark, blinking like a neon sign. When people look at me, they look at my birthmark. That's who I am—something odd and ugly—and I wish I could just disappear."

Rocky experiences a profound feeling of shame about a really rather mild disfigurement which he owns as an important and integral aspect of his Self. Someone else with a similar birthmark might neither own nor disown it, but simply leave it unowned: "Yeah, I have a birthmark. It's not very large and I just don't worry about it." Rocky's problems go deeper than the issue of his birthmark, but the transition from owning it to unowning it

153

defines a healthy direction for him. A healthier Self would have an identity independent of his birthmark, not defined by it.

With the stories of Dodge, May Lou, Maurice and Rocky before us, what can be said about the general trend: how do changes in ownership help? Coming to own something can help you to be comfortable with yourself—Dodge's cool demeanor for example. It can also help you to take responsibility for yourself and effect change—May Lou's aggression toward her kids. Disowning an attribute you initially own can be helpful by triggering a reaction against control—Maurice's compulsive gambling. And, when both owning and disowning are problematic, the characteristic in question is better off unowned—Rocky's birthmark.

Why all the variety instead of some general sweeping rule that it *always* helps to take ownership, or that it *always* helps to relinquish ownership? This is just more testimony that our life of thoughts and feelings is a world of nuances. Where the borders of the Self are best placed depends not on some broad principle but on a delicate negotiation within ourselves (perhaps with professional help), where we search for a Self-definition that will serve our well-being. The most important thing is to recognize how much elbow room we have in drawing the borders of our Selves.

Summary

Every person is, in part, his own project, and makes himself.
—Abraham Maslow

We react not only to the world and external stimuli but also to our Selves. The notion of second-order effects helps us to understand how. We can be afraid of our anger, or ashamed of our fear, or angry at our helplessness. We can have thoughts and feelings about our thoughts and feelings. This capacity to pull back and experience our Selves as object is generally healthy. Still, sometimes second-order effects cause us as much pain, and contribute as much to counterintentional behavior, as do first-order effects.

Not only can we pull back and observe ourselves, we can pull back even further and observe our own self-observations and reactions. Taking this third-order perspective helps us to direct and control second-order effects that make trouble for us. We could pullback further yet—fourth-order effects and beyond. But the usefulness of the idea fades beyond the third order as we become more and more removed from our direct experience of the world and of our Selves.

Even second-order effects raise a puzzling issue: "Who am I, really? Am I my Self who is encountering the world? Or am I the Self who is encountering myself encountering the world? Or what?" In everyday life we don't usually spend a lot of time agonizing over these questions because some general rules (my Self lives mostly inside my skin) and some habitual personal exceptions (a childhood teddy bear) give us practical answers.

However, when blocks become a problem, it's useful to recognize how negotiable the boundaries of the Self can be. The Self is a construction which we have developed over time as a result of our experiences, and which continues to develop throughout our lifespan. We consider different objects and characteristics owned (part of), disowned (alien to), or unowned (irrelevant) in relation to our essential Self. The status of anything may change over time, and so change the Self/Not-Self-boundary. Indeed, changes in ownership have profound consequences for self-acceptance, sense of responsibility, and self-control.

Acknowledging the operation of higher order effects and thinking of the Self as a construction are helpful in understanding and managing block. Still, their great advantage is also the most difficult thing about them: their very adaptability and usefulness also mean that they leave an awful lot open for interpretation. This sort of elbow room can be scary. It creates responsibilities for choice, meaning-making and self-determination.

ThinkAbouts

What does all this mean to you? *How might you continue to think about the ideas presented in this chapter?*

• When your thoughts or feelings *about* yourself are making you uncomfortable or unhappy, try to remember that human beings are built with the capacity for self-reflection for a good reason. Our ability to observe ourselves—and even to "step outside" ourselves and treat ourselves with some objectivity—allows us to learn from our mistakes and successes.

• Practice recognizing your "second-order" experiences, your reactions to some aspect of your Self rather than of the World. With a little attention you can get quite good at evaluating your situation at the first-, second-, and even the third-order levels. Drawing escalating "circles of causation" for your particular situation is a useful way to organize this effort.

• The boundaries of what is You and what is Not You aren't always clear, especially when you are feeling alienated from your own feelings or thoughts. Try to identify your relationship to your counterintentional behavior. Do you Own it? Do you Disown it? Do you Unown it?

• Just as the ambiguities of hidden force interpretations require you to think critically, and insight is most useful as an ongoing process rather than as an end product, so the changeable boundaries of the Self challenge you to constructively define and redefine them as you grow and learn and live.

Chapter 6

BLOCK LOCK

How Forces Enthrall Us

Sloan and his ten-year-old daughter, Annie, are walking back towards their car past all the little storefronts on Main Street. After a quick trip to pick up a newspaper and some bagels, they are heading home where Sloan's wife and son are waiting. Annie, holding Sloan's hand but straining to skip ahead, suddenly pulls up short in front of the hobby shop. She has spotted the display of new art materials in the window, and insists on going inside to look at them. Art is Annie's favorite activity. As she said one night to her parents' great amusement, "Art is my passion."

Sloan was afraid of this. He doesn't want to dally, and he dreads the thought of spending a half hour resisting his daughter's pleas to buy this or that. Annie is insistent though, and Sloan is loath to discourage so serious an interest, given his frequent frustration with his son Oliver, whose interest in model building seems to be so fickle.

Finally, Sloan suggests that Annie can go into the store for ten minutes—"And ONLY ten minutes, young lady!"—while he waits outside or browses in the bookstore next door. They agree.

After Annie happily enters the hobby store, Sloan loiters on the sidewalk for a few minutes. He gazes into the bookstore window and then wanders in, as much to escape the chilly wind as anything else. He has no particular errand. He isn't looking for any particular book. On the contrary, he's anxious to get home. Still, he has nothing else to do, so he starts to wander the aisles. He finds an attractive display featuring a book that was reviewed in last week's newspaper. He picks up the book and starts to browse through it. He notices that the display also includes other books by the same author, and books by other authors about the same topic. Before long Sloan is no longer just passing the time; he is quite enthralled by his reading.

Fifteen minutes later he hears his daughter approach. "Oh, there you are, Daddy!" Sloan continues to browse, aware that Annie is waiting, but captivated by the display of books. "I'm all done, Daddy!" says Annie, hooking a hand into his coat pocket. And in a minute, "Come on, Daddy! Let's goooooo!" "Soon, honey," he says, spying another title that looks interesting. Finally, Annie manages to drag him, literally, away from his reading. Even before they reach the street, she is regaling him with descriptions of the wonders in the hobby shop, and Sloan is asking her all about them without a second thought to the book display that had so gripped him a moment before.

Let's examine Sloan's experience. He lingers in the bookstore even though he knows his daughter is getting impatient, his wife and son are at home waiting for their bagels, and he has been looking forward all week to a leisurely morning around the house. There must be strong pro-lingering forces at work to overcome these obvious anti-lingering forces.

But there's something odd about these pro-lingering forces. They seem to operate differently when Sloan is *not* involved in browsing than when he *is*. When Sloan enters the bookstore, the books have little "pull." Unlike Annie's enthusiasm for the art supplies, Sloan feels pretty neutral. However, once actually engaged in browsing, Sloan discovers that the activity has a very

160

strong "grip." Once enthralled, he finds it difficult to break away. As soon as Annie drags him away, however, the spell is broken. He happily responds to her conversation about her discoveries. Reading has lost its grip on him and returns to its original status as a low-pull activity.

How can we understand why browsing exerts a stronger force when Sloan is doing it than when he is not? The notions of "pull" and "grip" can help. "Pull" describes the drawing force of an activity when we are not engaged in it, while "grip" describes its holding force once we *are* engaged in it. For example, art-related activities are high-pull and high-grip for Annie. When she is not engaged in them, they draw her, and once she is engaged they hold her. Standing out in the chilly wind and waiting for his daughter is, for Sloan, a low-pull/low-grip conduct, neither attractive nor engaging.

Let's look at Sloan's son, Oliver. His model-building is a high-pull/low-grip activity. Oliver is drawn to plastic do-it-yourself models of ships and airplanes, and he begs for nothing else on his birthday. He knows every model on the toy store shelves, and spends his allowance buying new ones. But once he gets them home and starts the meticulous work of putting them together, he always loses interest. His room is littered with half-finished hulls and fusilages. Model-building attracts him strongly when he is not actually engaged in it but doesn't hold him for long once he begins.

Sloan's experience with his bookstore browsing shows us yet another combination: low-pull/high-grip. The activity held him strongly once he got started, although he was not especially drawn to it beforehand. Indeed, situations where grip is greater than pull are quite common. If you've ever blown an evening watching TV or reading a mystery novel, sat on the edge of your seat through the ninth inning of a baseball game, or worked an hour overtime on an interesting project without realizing it, then you know the very commonplace nature of a gripping activity. In each of these cases, you might have been only slightly drawn to it initially. But once in, it's hard to get out—even hard to be pulled out, as Annie had to pull Sloan out of the store.

Often our *enthrallment* in something can be a problem. Have you ever felt trapped in the activity, spellbound by it, stuck in it or consumed by it? To such an extent that you want out, but can't get out, despite your best intentions? An eating binge is an extreme case in point. Obsessive behavior is another. Sloan with his browsing has a mild case of the same problem.

The grip-greater-than-pull combination gives another twist to our discussion of counterintentional behavior. We call it "the thrall effect," and activities that grab us like that we call "thralls." This handy terminology conveys the phenomenon's double edge: the grip-greater-than-pull effect can enrapture us. But it can enslave us too.

The notion of thralls helps us to understand how we can get captured by an activity to the point of block. Let's first look into thralls of different sorts and then check out the mechanics of the thrall effect. Finally, we'll explore how to use our understanding of the thrall effect to gain some control over counterintentional behavior.

The Thrall of It All

Isa Whitney . . . was much addicted to opium. The habit grew upon him, as I understand, from some foolish freak when he was at college, for having read DeQuincey's description of his dreams and sensations, he had drenched his tobacco with laudenum in an

attempt to produce the same effects. He found, as so many more
have done, that the practice is easier to attain than to get rid of.
—Sir Arthur Conan Doyle

Life may not always be full of thrills, but it is certainly full of thralls. Some are precious, some pernicious. And still others are totally ordinary. To map the landscape of thralls more clearly, let's speak of "peak thralls," "pit thralls" and "plain thralls."

"Peak thralls" are thralls that are especially delightful or productive. Intense involvement in a project, a sports match, a conversation, the making of a work of art, bird watching, or any like activity can be an absorbing and often creative experience. In such cases, you often seem to merge with the activity, getting so caught up in it that everything else falls away.

In general, there is little risk in peak thralls, although they may occasionally keep us from other matters that need attention. Only if a peak thrall becomes chronically distracting, or if it is just a way of avoiding other more important activities, it may be a serious problem. For instance, college students may become avid bridge players not just to enjoy bridge but to evade studying. In such cases, the peak is really a pit.

"Pit thralls" are activities that capture people contrary to their best intentions and do serious mischief. Chronic bridge playing is a special case, but binges of all sorts are the classic examples. The alcoholic who falls off the wagon, the dieter who gorges on ice cream, smokers trying to quit who suddenly find themselves chain-smoking as though to catch up, all show the captivating power of pit thralls.

Of course, we've talked about problems like this in earlier chapters. What does the idea of thralls add to the picture? It adds an important twist to a straight "strong forces" interpretation. The formula of grip-greater-than-pull gives a clearer sense of the dynamics of addictions. Addicts often describe being able to go along okay for some time—because the pull of the problematic activity, weaker than the grip, does not capture them. However, once they slip into the activity, they can't easily escape: the grip is very hard to break. The grip-greater-than-pull analysis also explains a well-known approach to controlling addictions. Alcoholics, for example, are warned to be wary of the first drink, "the fatal glass of beer." Why? Pull is easier to deal with than grip, so it's wise to focus on coping with the pull. If you can resist the pull of that first beer, you won't have to deal with the terrible grip of a bender.

Finally, between peak and pit thralls there are "plain thralls." Getting started doing the dishes may be a little hard, but, once you're started, the activity flows along. Reading the newspaper at breakfast, you may forget your cereal for a few minutes. You carry on happily spading the garden for hours. In contrast to pit thralls and peak thralls, plain thralls are pretty easily broken. A ringing phone, a glance at the clock, a question from someone else may snap you out of your thrall and into an entirely different activity.

Are these plain thralls just a quirk of human psychology? No, they do an important job for us. Plain thralls help us to keep organized. They hold us gently in our current activities, preventing our flitting from one activity to another and never getting anything done.

Imagine, for instance, that you have several more or less equally attractive activities that you could pursue at the moment—reading a novel, vacuuming the rug (attractive because you hate those dust bunnies!), watching TV. Now suppose there were no thrall effect. As you think of the novel, you pick it up and sit down to read. However, while turning a page a minute later, you happen to notice the TV in the corner of the room. That reminds you of a TV program you like, so you turn on the TV. After all, with no thrall effect, the grip of the book is no greater than its pull, so you are easily lured away by another activity of equal pull. On the way back from the TV, you notice a piece of lint on the rug. That reminds you of your campaign against lint, so, forgetting about the TV, you get out the vacuum cleaner. You'll never finish the novel at this rate!

Now contrast the case where plain thralls are on the job. When you open the book, you are at least mildly captured by it. Although you notice the TV while turning a page, you don't get lured away, because the grip of your current reading, stronger than its original pull, keeps you centered on the book. Of course, the grip is still gentle; a phone call or door bell would draw you away easily. But that slight edge of grip over pull keeps you constant instead of flighty.

So, like all force phenomena discussed earlier in this book, thralls usually have positive effects. They stabilize our everyday behavior and, in the case of peak thralls, keep us thoroughly embedded in activities that offer special rewards. However, as with other force phenomena, there's a downside; pit thralls and those occasions where peak thralls prove too distracting for your own good. Then you get counterintentional behavior. This downside gives plenty of reason to understand better how thralls work and what can be done to manage them.

The Clockwork of Thralls

Why do thralls operate as they do? To put it another way, what is the clockwork of thralls—the psychological springs that unwind and gears that engage to make thralls happen? To answer the question, let's take a look at three topics: why grip is greater than pull, how thralls come and go, and what sorts of activities enthrall us.

Why Grip Is Greater Than Pull

Here I am in the midst of the latest James Bond novel, and, although I have important work to do, I can't seem to put the book down. Understandable.

Then the phone rings. Annoyed, I answer it and talk for five minutes. After I hang up, I think about what to do. Return to the novel? It's the same novel I was reading five minutes ago, the same chapter, same caper, same cliffhanger. Yet now the important work pulls me more.

Not so understandable! I'm glad to get on with my work. But why do the work forces "win" now when they couldn't before? Apparently, it's not the case that a force is a force is a force. The strengths of the various forces in my situation *changed* during my five-minute break. Why aren't forces consistent?

Well, one reason seems to be that when you shift your attention towards or away from a particular activity, it is as though you are moving from one psychological environment to another. Remember the circle of causation, where a person (1) encounters situations, (2) perceives them, (3) which evokes forces, (4) which prompt a response. Naturally the forces evoked change when the situation you directly encounter changes. The environment of being-in-the-activity gives rise to different forces than the environment of not-being-in-the-acitivty. Take the James Bond example. Sure, I'm at a cliffhanger in the novel. But the cliffhanger is more vivid, the dilemma more precarious, the fate

166

of the world more fateful while I'm actually reading. So pro-reading forces are on a roll when I am in the middle of a paragraph, and other forces get rolling in their place when my attention shifts.

There's another factor. Deep involvement in something leaves little room in your mind for considering alternative activities. So alternative forces aren't activated. In psychological terms, this is a matter of "cognitive load." We have only a limited capacity for keeping multiple things in mind at the same time. When occupied with one activity, we don't have much mental room left to imagine what else we might be doing. Here I am reading the James Bond novel. It occurs to me in passing that I ought to be pursuing my important, and even fairly interesting, work. But I can't seem to concentrate on the idea of getting to work. It fades out of my mind, and I'm deep into the next chapter before I know it.

In other words, the grip-greater-than-pull effect gets its strength from a double whammy: First, the immediate activity is typically the most salient thing we encounter. So any attractive forces that it has get fully activated—its grip is strengthened. Second, the more enthralling the immediate activity, the more we attend to it. So the less mental space we have for other activities that might draw us away—their pulls are weakened.

How Thralls Come and Go

Let's tell this story in terms of Sean, a fortyish, overweight, middle-level executive who has a cigar habit. Sean has decided to cut down. He decides he'll just resist the impulse to smoke. Let's see how his plan goes.

Walking down the street on the way to work, Sean seems safe;

cigars hardly enter his mind. But then he passes a cigar store and in he goes, a knee-jerk reflex. The next day, Sean decides to avoid temptation and takes a different route to work. But then at the office, a new and happy father offers him a cigar: he can't say no. Sean has the habit of enjoying a smoke after dinner. The desire comes on like a tide as soon as Sean settles in front of the TV for the evening news. He lights up.

Even other times of day are not truly safe. Sunday morning, Sean finds himself lounging quietly in the back yard. The image of a long, rich cigar happens to occur to him. He's not doing anything else, so, once the idea presents itself, it won't go away. That cigar floats in front of his eyes. Pretty soon, hardly aware that he has made a decision, he finds himself on his way inside to get one.

In other words, despite his best intentions, situations *capture* Sean. But this doesn't mean that Sean is completely helpless all the time. Thralls come and go. Just as a number of circumstances get Sean into a smoking thrall, a number get him out. After the evening TV news and cigar, he plays with his kids for a while and doesn't smoke then because he knows it's bad for them. He may smoke on the way to the office, but dumps his cigar at the door, because he knows cigar smoke is not appreciated there. And often, after a long, slow cigar, Sean has simply had enough—he is satisfied and doesn't want any more.

Sean's pattern is pretty typical of the way thralls come and go in everyday life. We get into thralls through a combination of chance and habit. Chance creates occasions where a thought that's initially resistible gets stimulated beyond the point of resistance, as with Sean's passing the store or happening to think of cigars while lounging in the back yard. Habits, such as Sean's nightly cigar-with-the-news, create a special vulnerability at certain times or in certain settings.

And we get out of thralls because the grip lessens, as when Sean is satiated, or when other forces powerful enough to break the thrall come into play, like Sean's concern for his kids' health.

Sean's story describes getting into and out of a pit thrall. But it's also worth remembering that we often deliberately put ourselves into peak and plain thralls. We sit down with the novel and get enthralled *intentionally*, to relax before bedtime. We go to the movies or the baseball game, turn to our most interesting project at work, even sometimes hope to fall in love, in full consciousness that we are committing ourselves to gripping experiences. Indeed, a person might well feel that life is not as rich as it should be without truly enthralling activities to enjoy.

What Enthralls Us

Whatever attracts us has the potential to enthrall us. And the more the attraction, the deeper the thrall. Remember, there are basic reasons for the grip-greater-than-pull effect. Because of those basic reasons, whatever attracts us is likely to enthrall us at least somewhat. There are exceptions. Recall, for instance, Sloan's son Oliver earlier in the chapter, who loved to get model airplanes but soon lost interest in actually assembling them— high-pull but low-grip. But this is an exception and not the rule.

Beyond the general rule, what enthralls us varies a lot from person to person, because what attracts us varies a lot. There are certainly common denominators. Falling in love is an attraction and a thrall that most of us are happy to experience at one time or another—"the tender trap." But there's enormous variety too: one person takes great joy in collecting etchings, another in collecting butterflies, another in collecting stamps. None of the three feels any special attraction to the other's enthusiasms. Accidents of personal history, personal growth and personal taste make an activity enthralling for a particular individual at a certain time of life. Later or earlier, elsewhere or for another person, the story can be very different.

It's not the job of the thrall notion—or of Force Theory in general—to explain why particular individuals get hooked on one thing and not another. Why, for instance, one person collects stamps and another etchings. Individual responses to different forces is an aspect of the human condition. It *is* the job of the thrall notion to clarify the nature of the grip-greater-than-pull phenomenon—and to help us deal with it better.

Managing Thralls

So now we *understand* something about the clockwork of thralls. But wouldn't it be even better to be less *enthralled* by our thralls? Perhaps understanding how thralls work can help us to figure out how to manage them so that they don't leave us stuck in counter-intentional behaviors.

When we think of managing thralls, we probably think first of managing *pit* thralls—thralls that block us into an activity despite our efforts to escape it. And we'll certainly take a look at these, below. However, another important aspect of managing thralls involves trying to get *into* a *peak* thrall, rather than trying to get *out* of a *pit* thrall. Wouldn't it be great, for example, if washing the dishes could hold your attention with the same grip as watching TV does? Understanding the mechanics of thralls can help us get into desirable activities, as well as helping us get out of undesirable activities.

In general, the same sorts of strategies that apply to any troublesome pattern of forces help us in managing thralls. After all, a thrall situation may well involve the kinds of forces discussed in previous chapters: strong forces, hidden forces or second-order forces. However, thralls have that additional oddity of grip greater than pull, which gives their management a special twist. Remembering the circle of causation, thralls seem to invite approaches that focus on the point of encounter (exposure to a thrall stimulus) and the point of reaction (your response to that stimulus). Let's see how.

Avoid Getting Into a Thrall: Deal With Pull

Emma is a recovering alcoholic. She used to stop by every night at a particular liquor store on her way home from work. Her first few attempts to cease drinking failed, each time because she felt the usual tug of the store as she drove home, and automatically pulled over, went in and bought something. Emma's AA sponsor suggested that she change her route home from work so that she would stay out of the way, literally, of temptation. Together they mapped a new route, and they taped the map onto her dashboard. Taking the new route home helped Emma stay sober.

A strategic application of will succeeded for Emma where sheer will power failed. She managed to resist drinking not by escaping the thrall's grip, but by dodging the thrall before she was pulled in. Remember that dealing with the pull of a thrall is invariably easier than dealing with its grip.

Emma's strategy was to manage her situation at the point of her encounter with the world, avoiding a situation that drew her into a thrall. She stayed out of reach of the thrall's pull and hence its grip. We mentioned a similar example in an earlier chapter: keeping the potato chips in the kitchen cupboard rather than on the counter. The old saying, ''Out of sight, out of mind,'' can be a thrall-breaking prescription.

Of course, you can't always avoid the situations that provoke thralls. Norman, for example, found it hard to quit smoking partly because his wife smoked. Even when he could go all day at the office without a cigarette, his resolve failed him once his wife lit up after dinner. Since he couldn't avoid an encounter with temptation, he tried another tack, substituting a different response than smoking. Norman bought a small handsome lacquered box and some sugarless menthol candies. He placed the box with the candies in it on the side table in the dining room. Whenever his wife reached for a cigarette, Norman reached for a menthol. Having this alternative helped him to resist smoking.

Norman's wife, Nell, was so inspired by his success that she developed her own tactic for avoiding the pull of another temptation, eating between meals. Although Nell was trying to stick to a diet, it had been almost impossible for her to avoid encountering temptation because there was always food in the fridge for her family. So she taped her weight chart and a particularly unflattering picture of herself on the door of the refrigerator. This changed her encounter with the world. Whenever she made a move for the leftovers, she encountered her weight chart and photo, warning her off.

Break Out of a Thrall: Deal With Grip

Joy had a terrible time limiting her television watching in the evening. She would turn on the TV at 6:30 just to watch the news, but then she couldn't seem to turn it off. Sometimes she watched until she fell asleep. Her will power seemed useless once she had begun. She didn't want to give up viewing the news, but she decided that she had to do something to break out of the grip of the television thrall once she fell into it.

172

So Joy got strategic. She attached her TV to an electric light timer that would automatically shut it off at 8:00 P.M. When the TV went off, she found her "trance" broken and could turn her attention to other things. Joy's strategy helped her to get out of her pit thrall by breaking her perceptual contact with the enthralling activity. The TV timer did for Joy what Annie did for her father in our story at the opening of this chapter. When Annie literally dragged her father out of the bookstore, she broke his perceptual contact with the enthralling situation.

Of course, Joy's thrall-breaking measure was hardly foolproof. She could simply reset the timer or turn the TV back on when it shut off. But it was easier for her to decide intelligently what to do once the TV was off, because then she only had to deal with the pull of TV watching, not its grip.

Get Into Desirable Thralls: Turn the Clockwork to Your Advantage

Ernie says he loves to write. But, for someone who loves to write, he has an awfully hard time getting down to work. He puts off starting, although he knows that, once writing, he usually finds himself "on a roll."

So Ernie gets strategic about his situation. He discovers that the best way for him to get down to work is not just to jump in. The thought of jumping in fills him with dread and makes him procrastinate all the more. Rather, he has better luck getting started by simply "putting himself in the way of it." He seats himself in the middle of writing-related sights, sounds and objects: sharpened pencils, humming computer, steaming coffee, comfortable desk chair. He gets nicely settled—but doesn't try to write. Instead he just peruses what he wrote at his last sitting. As he reads, thoughts about the text occur to him, either revisions or new text. Almost without intending to, he becomes captured by the activity and finds himself deeply engaged.

Ernie capitalized on the clockwork of thralls to help him to get into a thrall, just as the people in the earlier examples used the clockwork to avoid or escape from a thrall. Working strategically at the point of his encounter with the world, Ernie actually started up the circle of causation characteristic of pit thralls—but in the service of a peak thrall instead.

A different strategy for getting into a peak thrall appears in the case of Emilia, a would-be runner who *thinks* about going running much more often than she gets herself to the track. She always enjoys running once she's doing it, and she is always glad she went. But, when she is sitting peacefully on her couch, running seems like it will take too much energy. In those placid moments, she can't simply will herself to get up and go.

But Emilia discovers that she can, by an act of will, tap her foot. Now, whenever she finds herself merely *thinking* about running when she should be *doing* something about it, Emilia begins to tap her foot. The trivial physical activity reminds her of how bodily motion feels and of the rhythm of running. The small activity makes running seem more possible, and she even feels that she has already begun. Before long, Emilia is tapping both feet, then getting up from the couch, and then heading for the track.

Emilia gets her thrall going by working first at the point of *reaction* rather than the point of *encounter*. By foot-tapping, an easy reaction to her reluctant impulse to run, Emilia evokes more running-related stimuli (activity, warm muscles, rhythm), which in turn provoke a pro-running reaction, and so on.

Ernie could take a clue from this variation on his strategy. He sometimes sits down in a writing situation and still feels blocked.

Well, he could work on his reaction rather than his encounter. He might try something like "freewriting." In this technique, recommended by some writing coaches, he would pick up a pencil and write whatever occurs to him, non-stop, purely for the sake of the activity, without any planning or editing. The activity of freewriting sets up a writing-related situation (verbal thinking, attention-to-task, etc.) that often spirals into more thoughtful and systematic writing.

Conclusion

Let's summarize. A thrall is a force situation that we experience differently from the "inside" than from the "outside": its grip is greater than its pull. So thralls are easier to *stay* out of in the first place than to *get* out of once you're in. Overall, the thrall effect is a good thing. It stabilizes our behavior, keeping us from flitting from one thing to another. But when our behavior gets stabilized on something we don't want to be doing—or when we can't seem to settle into something that we *do* want to be doing—then we find ourselves in a counterintentional dilemma.

So what makes thralls hard to get out of once you're in? We get stuck in thralls because of a self-sustaining interplay between the conditions we encounter and our reactions to those conditions. At its worst, this produces a vicious circle, such as an addiction, and at best, a luscious circle, such as being in love (the requited, not the unrequited, kind). Most thralls, though, are just routine—neither especially problematic nor especially enjoyable.

Strategic applications of the will can go far in making or breaking a thrall. Occasionally, successful interventions get made at the points of *perceptions* and *forces* in the circle of causation. The most effective interventions, however, focus on the points of *encounter* and *reaction*. Thrall is a useful concept for self-management: thinking in terms of thrall-avoiding, thrall-breaking and thrall-making strategies can help us manage our counterintentional behavior when sheer will power fails.

Still, there are times when seemingly well-chosen strategies don't do the job. Despite good stategizing, Emma could tie one on, Norman could light one up, and Emilia could degenerate into a couch potato. They might find that, no matter what they try, they can't "make" themselves behave as they wish. They might continue to be astonished and mystified by the stubborness and power with which they subvert their own intentions.

When thralls resist our best thrall-busting efforts, what's going on? It could be that we have simply underestimated the strength of the forces at work, or that we have overlooked a relatively simple hidden force. These are common errors, just as likely in a thrall situation as in any other force situation. We can deal with them effectively using the sorts of strategies discussed in previous chapters. But thralls also can prove stubborn for two very particular reasons. What are they? And how do we deal with *them*?

First of all, some thralls have more to do with your mental world than your physical world. You may fall into mooning over an absent lover even though there are hardly any reminders around. You may find yourself reliving an embarrassing moment over and over, wishing that you had handled it differently. When your son calls from the kitchen, "Mooom! Where's the leftover potato salad?" you may find yourself tormented by a bad case of the munchies for the next two hours, even though potato salad was the furthest thing from your mind until then, and even though the actual potato salad in question was finished off by your spouse the night before.

In other words, sometimes the vicious circle that sustains a thrall involves mental encounters—images in our minds—rather than only physical encounters—stimuli in the world. The adage mentioned earlier, "Out of sight, out of mind," is all very well, but what about the retort, "Absence makes the heart grow fonder?" These sorts of psychological stimuli and reactions are sometimes more difficult to detect and often more difficult to manage. After all, while you can do much to avoid encounters with physical situations, it's harder to avoid your own mind, since you carry it around with you! Telling yourself to put something out of your mind may have as much of an effect as saying, "Don't think of pink elephants."

One thing you *can* try to do in such situations is to avoid physical follow-through. Just because you're dreaming of the potato salad doesn't mean you have to stuff your face with whatever's handy. Just because you're dreaming of your absent lover doesn't mean that you have to mope around the house all weekend. Often, the answer to mental thralls seems to be not so much *breaking* the troublesome thrall as *making* a "counter-thrall" that distracts you—getting involved in something else such as a good book, a compelling movie, interesting work, a friend's problems instead of your own. Such maneuvers are not likely to entirely vanquish deep preoccupations such as an absent lover, but they do lessen the effects and foster a greater sense of self-control. And they may solve the potato salad problem entirely!

When you're trying to deal with thralls, another rather different problem sometimes comes up. Joy's TV watching, which she treated as a simple thrall, may not be so simple after all. Joy may be watching so much TV because she's depressed. If so, she may successfully limit her TV watching only to find herself overeating or experiencing some other expression of her depression. Treating her depression might be more appropriate than treating her TV watching. But why is Joy so depressed? Perhaps because she is genetically prone to a neurochemical imbalance. Or perhaps because she is lonely. She might be lonely because she needs to improve her social skills—which won't have the chance to improve if she sits at home all the time watching TV. Or perhaps her social skills are poor in the first place because her predisposition towards depression contributed to a socially isolated childhood. And there could be big second-order effects in Joyce's situation. She may be depressed by her own isolation, and feel that she must be unlovable or she wouldn't be sitting home alone night after night and watching TV. In fact, if it weren't for the company of the TV, she could become *morbidly* depressed. So breaking her TV thrall might backfire.

Speculations like this about Joy make it easier to understand why a one-shot strategic thrall-breaking technique might fail, or cause more problems than it solves. Thinking in terms of a TV thrall may vastly oversimplify her situation if Joy's behavior arises from many interconnected factors. In other words—surprise, surprise—blocks can be pretty complicated.

Earlier we warned against the view that *all* psychological problems are deep, involving tangles of hidden forces. Many blocks are quite straightforward—strong forces at work, easily seen second-order effects, and so on. Also, we emphasized that occasionally deep problems allow rather straightforward solutions or partial solutions. But situations like Joy's remind us that sometimes blocks *do* involve tangles of hidden forces and *do* resist straightforward solutions.

The next chapter offers some help in navigating the maze of possibilities. There, we explore the boggling complexity of the multiplicity of forces that constantly influence us. How are we to make sense of them all?

ThinkAbouts

*What does all this mean to you? How might you continue
to think about the ideas presented in this chapter?*

• Behaviors can "pull" you to engage in them—making them
hard to resist—and "grip" you once you are engaged—making
them hard to escape. Try to notice the different pulls and grips of
various activities.

• When you discover that an activity's grip is greater than its
pull, admit that you have encountered a "thrall." You may be
pleased, as when you realize you have fallen in love, or you may
be distressed, as when you realize your gambling has gotten out
of control. In any case, identifying your situation as a thrall is an
important step in figuring out how you might want to deal with it.

• The points of *encounter* and *reaction* on the circle of causation
are especially good intervention points in trying to manage a
problematic thrall. For example, try minimizing your encounters
with temptation, or substituting an alternative reaction to it, and
thus evade the clutches of a gripping enthrallment.

• When you find yourself blocked *out* of a desirable activity
rather than blocked *in* to an undesirable one, you can turn the
grip-is-greater-than-pull characteristic of the thrall effect to your
advantage. Once you begin, it won't be so hard to continue. So
be strategic: get yourself to take that first step, make that first
move, and trust that the grip of the activity will help keep you
going once you get on track.

Chapter 7

BLOCKS ON ALL SIDES

Navigating the Landscape of Forces

Laid off during a reorganization, Saul has been unemployed for seven months. And of course he hates it. Money is tight and savings are dwindling. Every job interview is an ordeal, rejection is painful, and the future is uncomfortably uncertain. Despite his experience, skills, and a good job record, Saul's efforts to find another good position have been futile.

Then one day Saul gets a call offering him a job at one of the companies where he interviewed. The money is good and the job description matches his skills. But just as he's about to jump at the chance, he remembers a problem: his interviews at this place left him with serious reservations about the guy who would be his boss. It's not just that Saul and Mr. Kemp didn't hit it off—Kemp was exactly the sort of person that Saul knew would drive him nuts. Saul enjoys a lot of independence in his work and feels he works best that way. Kemp struck him as a meddlesome fellow who might even say things like, "Because I'm your boss, that's why!"

So Saul asks the caller for 24 hours to think about it. She says fine. But, she warns, they have a promising second-choice candidate whom they are eager to call should Saul decline.

Every minute of the next 24 hours is torture for Saul. He can't make a decision. "Take the job . . . Keep looking . . . Take the job. . . Keep looking." Each time he thinks he has decided one way, he remembers its drawbacks and the alternative begins to look good again. He feels blocked and unable to make a choice.

What's worse, it seems that the more he thinks about it, the more complex the decision becomes. It's not just a question of whether he'll be able to stand his boss. Other issues come in to play, such as how long his finances can support a continued search, whether he and his wife can start a family this year as they had hoped, where his career is headed, whether he is destined to end up in a job he hates just like his father, and on and on.

Saul is up all night. Even as he watches the 24-hour deadline approach, and then slip by, he is still painfully unable to decide. Finally, six hours after the deadline, Saul picks up the phone to make the call, unsure even as he dials what his choice will be. Before he can say one thing or the other, the company agent speaks. "I'm sorry Mr. Allen, but when we hadn't heard from you after 24-hours, we gave the position to the other candidate."

Saul's situation probably sounds familiar even if you've never experienced the same misfortune. Whenever you can't decide which suit to wear, or what entree to order, or whether or not you can put off doing the laundry for one more day, you feel torn between competing alternatives.

When such things happen, you, like Saul, are experiencing yet another form of block. That's what makes Saul's situation worth special attention. Saul isn't just blocked *in* or blocked *out*, force configurations already discussed. Rather, he is blocked *between*. He isn't dealing with one source of forces, but a number of different sources of forces operating simultaneously in complex interaction.

In particular, Saul's job opportunity generates both positive and negative forces: He does want the paycheck coming in. But he doesn't want to work for someone he can't stand. The path of continuing his job search also arouses a positive force—he does want a job that's right for him. And a negative force—he doesn't want to further strain his already strained resources. Whichever position he leans toward, Saul becomes vividly aware of its downside and shies away. Saul is indeed blocked *between*.

Force Landscapes

We can imagine Saul existing in a sort of force landscape. As he vacillates between one or the other alternative, he walks through his landscape, encountering different forces. Not only does he encounter simple "pros" and "cons," which push and pull him directly, but he stumbles into the web of different force contexts, all interrelated: his job decision interacts with his financial concerns which interact with his desire to start a family which interact with his feelings about his father, and on and on. How complicated!

The same complexity is not hard to find in anyone. If you think carefully about the many factors that influence your behavior moment to moment, you'll be impressed at how complex an image emerges. You go along, encountering, perceiving and responding to your world and to your self. Forces arise and subside, attract and repel you from all over the place. Few forces exist in isolation like oases in the middle of a desert—they're more like a dense forest, a colorful, complicated and diverse landscape. The notion of a personal force landscape seems to do justice to this in a way that naming one or two forces cannot.

The notion of a force landscape can help us to understand why we so often seem to repeat our frustrations and failures in our lives, contrary to our best intentions. As we move through our force landscapes, the view changes. What looks attractive from one spot may seem repellent from another. Each time Saul neared a final decision, it began to look less desirable. But as soon as he began to settle on the other alternative, history simply repeated itself. Perhaps, this is exactly what happens in larger repetitive behavior patterns, only in swings of months or years—for example, moving back and forth between wanting your independence and wanting a committed relationship, or alternating between risky gambling binges and periods of moderation.

So the image of force *landscapes* adds a new dimension to our understanding of force mechanisms. And it suggests some new ways to better manage the forces that determine our behavior.

Blocked Between

To begin to mine the idea of force landscapes, let's examine indecision. In general, indecision is a matter not of being blocked out of a course of action, or blocked into one, but blocked between. You can't seem to settle on either path. That's Saul's problem and a common problem for all of us.

What's going on in such situations? Let's examine some different cases.

The Classic Dilemma

In a dilemma in the classic dictionary sense, you are caught between two thoroughly undesirable options, or, in the vernacular, "caught between a rock and a hard place." In such situations, you're likely to vacillate or freeze. And both behaviors can be understood straightforwardly in force terms. As you move towards either option—even only in your mind—its disadvantages become more real and push you back. So you vacillate for awhile. As sooner or later you come to recognize that you can't easily take either path. You end up suspended motionless in the middle.

Saul's situation as originally described is a little more complicated than the classic dilemma, because both paths have marked positive as well as negative features. Still, the causes of blocked between are pretty much the same. The closer he comes to accepting the position, the worse it looks—daily interactions with Kemp are a chilling prospect. So Saul tentatively decides against the job and thinks about continuing his search. But the more carefully he looks at *this* option, the less viable *it* seems. Maybe he could put up with Kemp after all. And so on.

Blocked Between Desirables

At the opposite extreme from the classical dilemma is a second kind of blocked between, more mysterious but just as real. You find yourself blocked between two *desirable* directions. You like both rocky-road and mint-chocolate-chip ice cream—which flavor to order? You like both Janice and Mathilda—which girl to ask to the dance? You like both English and physics—which to choose as a major? Of course, we usually manage decisions about ice creams flavors readily enough. But the higher the stakes, the more painful such decisions can be.

For example, let's think about Saul again. This time, suppose that Saul receives two unexpected job offers within ten minutes—*both* for positions he would love to have. One position is at the Apex Company, an up-and-coming firm where Saul would have lots of independence, appreciation, good pay and great co-workers. The other position, with the larger, well-established Zenix Company, offers excellent salary and benefits, a very professional atmosphere around the office, and a strong ethic of mutual respect among colleagues. Saul finds himself unable to decide, blocked between different but equally attractive alternatives.

It's easy to understand why people get blocked between undesirables. After all, embracing either option in a classic dilemma is unpleasant. But why should it be so hard to choose between two desirables? Frustrated, we're likely to say to ourselves, "Just *choose* one, for goodness sake—*either* one!"

But it is not hard to understand the block in force landscape terms. Saul is stuck because, as he moves toward one option, he begins to regret losing what the other offers. "The grass is always greener on the other side of the fence."

There is even psychological research confirming the "grass is greener" effect. Research suggests that people place a higher value on something seen as a loss than on something seen as a gain. For example, when subjects in one experiment were asked to choose between two proposed treatment programs designed to deal with an epidemic outbreak of a rare and fatal disease, they were significantly more likely to choose a treatment plan that had a 67 percent chance of total success than one that had a 33 percent chance of total failure! But, of course, a 67 percent chance of success is the *same* as a 33 percent chance of failure! In cases of indecision between two desirables, you find yourself in a situation where, by definition, your choices must be roughly equally attractive. And yet, given the "grass is greener" principle, whichever way you turn, the loss of the one you plan to forgo tends to look bigger than the gain of the one you plan to choose.

The Apples and Oranges Factor

Besides the basic factor of forces in tension, another factor makes cases of blocked between hard to handle: their "apples and oranges" character. In situations like Saul's, you do not face simple choices between "apples, or no apples." Saul, for example, can easily choose between Kemp or not-Kemp (he chooses not-Kemp), or between money or no-money (he chooses money). But Saul may have a much harder time weighing the misery of working with Kemp against the satisfaction of a paycheck. Considering how many factors are involved in the whole situation, Saul may come to quite different conclusions moment-to-moment depending on where he focuses his attention.

Furthermore, the various aspects of his two alternatives interact with other decisions Saul wants to make, like whether or not he and his wife will start a family this year. With all this going on at once, Saul is facing not a simple yes-no choice, but different options with a maze of incomensurable consequences.

Getting Out From Blocked Between

People can and do use a number of strategies to resolve blocked-between situations. Often, you fall into these strategies only when driven by desperation—only when you've been thoroughly frustrated and finally end up using your will strategically as a last resort. While such strategies often are arrived at only under pressure, they *can* be used mindfully and intentionally closer to the beginning of the decision process.

First of all, you have to recognize that you *are* blocked between. This sounds simple, but is probably the main reason we

187

tend not to strategize until driven to do it. When your mind is occupied with the specific details of the decision at hand, it takes a change in perspective to consider the general nature of your bind. Then, you're in a position to strategize your way out.

Gathering more information. One of the simplest ways to resolve blocked-between situations—either by chance or by strategy—is through the infusion of new information. For instance, if Saul were to learn that Kemp is about to be transferred to the Dubuque offices, then he would have all he needs to resolve his dilemma. The hope in gathering more information is that something in the information will get you out of your bind.

Trying each option on for size. When we are vacillating between two options, we don't fully embrace either one. How are we to really know what we feel about an option if we never give it a chance, even hypothetically? Trying on each option for size can be very illuminating, letting you see how it looks and feel how it fits. To do this, you must imagine the decision to be already made and live with it for a while—an hour, or even a day. Then ask yourself seriously, ''What is it like, having made this choice? What are my reliefs and regrets? Can I live with this?'' This sort of role-playing sometimes gives you a chance to explore each alternative thoroughly, without being yanked away from your examination by the conflicting forces.

Flipping a coin. When caught between rocky-road and mint-chocolate- chip, why not flip a coin? After all, it hardly matters which flavor of ice cream wins out. To be sure, when major life issues are at stake, a random gamble seems inappropriate. But often, for more modest decisions, making the perfect choice between two nearly equal options doesn't seem worth the effort of a protracted decision process. Moreover, nothing absolutely compels you to accept the results of the flip and sometimes the flip will reveal hidden preferences that have not entered into your judgment. As Piet Hein wrote:

> Whenever you're called on to make up your mind,
> and you're hampered by not having any,
> the simplest way to solve the dilemma, you will find,
> is simply by flipping a penny.
>
> No—not so that chance shall decide the affair
> while you're passively standing there moping;
> but the moment the penny is up in the air,
> you suddenly know what you're hoping!

Creating new options. One of the most painful things about being blocked between is the feeling of being caught in a trap—no exit apart from one of the options before you. Often, however, this is more an assumption than a fact. It is usually possible to invent additional options to expand your elbow room—especially "left field" options. For example, Saul might decide to start his *own* business, or change careers, or go back to school. These possibilities are certainly not simple answers. They are each problematic in their own ways. Yet Saul may find in one of them a course of action he can commit himself to.

Synthesizing options. Similarly, it's a mistake to assume that the obvious options cannot be mixed or modified. Perhaps you can synthesize a hybrid option out of the best parts of the original options. For example, Saul, preferring not to work with Kemp, might be able to negotiate with his new employers, who seem eager to have him. He could be supervised by someone else, or he could be supervised by Kemp for only a short probationary period after which he'd be left on his own. Of course, options like these may not be possible. Still, too often we remain trapped in the choices we are given, when others would exist if only we would formulate and pursue them.

As effective as the above strategies can be, they are hardly foolproof. Often there is little time to gather more information, or none to be had. A simple coin-toss becomes three-out-of-five, or five-out-of-seven, or best-of-thirty-nine. Creative options may be unworkable despite your commitment to them, and synthesized alternatives may be unacceptable to those who must approve them. Still, rather than simply enduring counterintentional indecision, it's important to recognize your situation, distance yourself from it, use your will strategically, and work systematically at "getting out from blocked between."

Indecision by Design

Situations of blocked between often lead to decision by default: the course of events decides for you. This happened to Saul when his position was offered to the second-choice candidate because he didn't decide on time.

But decision by default is not always decision by accident. Sometimes the inability to decide is a response in itself, a hidden design for coping with difficult situations. When Sherry, a teenaged child of divorcing parents, is asked to choose which parent she will live with, she becomes blocked between her two options. She feels personally torn and does not want to hurt either parent. When, because of her indecision, the choice is finally taken out of her hands, she may feel relieved: "At least I won't have to choose!" What looks like an inability to decide may really be a refusal to decide.

Uncertain which choice to make anyway, Sherry avoids the

onus of deciding by refusing to decide. But sometimes there *is* a choice preferred deep down, which the person can't or won't make explicit. Suppose, for example, that Saul is more moved than he realizes by the fear that working under Kemp will lead to an unhappy lot like his father's. Because of this fear, Saul "deep down" wants to refuse the position. However, he doesn't feel able to make this preference explicit, even to himself, because it appears self-indulgent. Saul manages to put off the decision until it is apparently made for him—but it's really the one that he prefers "deep down."

Cases such as these show that indecision by hidden design may sometimes be a good thing. If indeed there is not much basis for choice in Sherry's case, perhaps she is better off letting others decide. Given the depth of Saul's concerns about Kemp, perhaps it is best for Saul to let the clock make the decision. On the other hand, what if the hidden forces at work are leading Sherry or Saul to neglect very real reasons why they *should* decide one way or another? The problem with hidden forces is that you can't weigh them in the balance in trying to arrive at a best judgment. Moreover, when hidden forces lead you towards a default decision, you are not exploring novel or synthesis options that might in fact prove much better than either of the choices you are avoiding.

So when you suspect that indecision may be "by design," it's often worthwhile to probe for the hidden forces at work and try to take them explicitly into account. Not so easily done, of course. It makes little sense to ask yourself what you *want* to have happen—if you knew *that*, you wouldn't be so blocked. Rather, you have to be more roundabout.

Instead, ask yourself what will happen when the situation gets decided by default. Saul could easily tell: he would lose the job.

191

Then he could go on to ask himself, "Do I *want, really*, to lose this job? And why?" Sherry might be able to forecast the likely decision if she couldn't decide. Or she might simply realize, "Whatever is decided, I won't have to face Mom or Dad with them knowing I picked the other." Bringing such factors to the surface could help Saul and Sherry take them into account. But, perhaps more important, it would free them from procrastination and let them think beyond the obvious options toward novel or synthesis options.

Repeating History

So far, we've explored the landscape of forces through the example of indecisiveness. But force landscapes do more mischief than just leaving us "blocked between" from time to time. For another kind of situation, consider Brenda's story.

Brenda's problem is that she falls into relationships with irresponsible men. At first, she loves their happy-go-lucky-character, so loose and laid back. It's a balm to her own slightly stiff way of looking at things. The trouble is, all that laidbackness eventually begins to get on her nerves. Trying to straighten out her happy-go-lucky fellow of the moment, she sooner or later drives him away. Not difficult to do because, after all, he's irresponsible.

Brenda sees the pattern. She swears off such relationships, but soon finds herself in another one. Why does history repeat itself? Why is Brenda blocked into a long-term cycle of behavior that she cannot seem to put behind her?

Remembering the landscape metaphor, perhaps we can blame *primrose paths* of psychological forces. At the beginning of such a path, the primroses are bright indeed. So, you take the path and move along it, looking to see what's there. Further down the path, the primroses begin to wilt. But you're already on the path. So you try to cope, dealing with new forces as best you can. Moment to moment, you always function more or less adaptively. But the fact is that the path runs downhill after the first few feet.

Let's walk Brenda's primrose path with her to see how it goes. At the beginning of a cycle, it's been a year since her last unfortunate affair. Her memories of it have faded. Happy-go-luck Geoffrey comes along and looks pretty good. The local forces say go with it for a bit. And who knows how things might turn out this time? Brenda does what looks like the rational thing, at least from a short term perspective. Brenda goes with it.

At first, she is happy that Geoffrey has moved in with her. She finds him entertaining, and he helps her break out of her routine. The local forces are all pro-Geoffrey. But after a while, Brenda catches up with herself. She begins to worry about the future. Will they marry? Should he work too? Is it fair that she's paying for the apartment and the groceries? Is this guy just a bum, clever though he is with a guitar, and even though he's had several poems published in literary magazines? What is she going to make out of her life, especially with him aboard?

Questions like this intrude because the force landscape has changed. At first such concerns didn't matter. After all, everything about the day-to-day relationship was fun and positive. But now that the relationship has endured for a while, she begins to look at it as anyone might look at an enduring thing. And, as an enduring thing, it looks different than it did as a fling. So Brenda again does the rational thing: instead of throwing the whole relationship away, she tries to salvage the situation by improving

193

it. She begins to encourage Geoffrey to get a steady job. Before long, she is nagging him, he is angry at her, and they seem to fight all the time.

At the end of the path, when they break up months later, Brenda recognizes her foolishness and again swears off such relationships. But that's at the end of the path, when the downside forces are immediate and vivid. At each spot along the way, she did the sensible thing, at least the "locally" sensible thing. When memories fade somewhat, as they will, she will be back near the beginning of the path and ready to do the locally rational thing again—when she meets an entertaining and creative guy, she may decide again to take a chance on him.

The sagas of Brenda and others in similar binds show us how a landscape of forces spread out over space and time can trap a person in counterintentional behavior as surely as a single force pit. And there's a moral for the strategic use of the will, as Brenda and the rest of us struggle to make sense of our counterintentional behavior and behave more in tune with our best intentions. It's not enough just to look at the immediate circumstances. We have to zoom back, seeking larger patterns of forces that sometimes leave us blocked between and the even larger patterns that lead us down primrose paths. And unlike, Brenda, we have to strategize from the lessons we learn, so we can break the cycle next time around.

Self-Sealing Situations

The landscape analogy can help us understand another puzzling human phenomenon. Sometimes the very actions we take to make things better only make things worse, and aggravate the block we are trying to break. For example, take Brenda at one point along her primrose path. It's not her intention to drive Geoffrey away. Yet, the harder Brenda tries to make her relationship with Geoffrey work, the closer she comes to destroying it.

Blocks like this emerge when disparate forces interact with one another to create what's often called a *self-sealing* system. An old story about elephants in the park illustrates the idea beautifully. A woman sits down for a rest on a park bench on a lovely summer day. At first, she pays little attention to the man sitting at the other end of the bench. But she soon notices that he is holding an umbrella, despite the fine weather. He opens it up every so often, holds it over his head for a few seconds, and then closes it again. Her curiosity grows, and she says to the man, "Excuse me, sir. I couldn't help noticing that it is a lovely day and yet you keep opening and closing your umbrella. Why are you doing that?" The man leans closer and replies in a conspiratorial voice, "Keeps the elephants away." "Elephants!" says the woman, "But there aren't any elephants in the park!" To which the man responds, with satisfaction, "Yes. It works quite well, doesn't it!"

The man with the umbrella has created an absurd and self-sealing understanding of his world: he wields his umbrella to test his remedy, and sure enough, there are no elephants. Analogously, in self-sealing blocks, the very actions you take to try to break out of them perversely seal them tighter. Such blocks aren't hard to come by. For example, you can picture someone who drinks to avoid his problems, thus interfering with his ability to deal with those very problems, not the least of which is that he drinks so much. Many phobias, as well, are based on—or at least abetted by—circular and self-sealing qualities. Suppose you're scared of elevators, believing that they're unsafe. Since elevators make you anxious, you stay away from them, which lessens your anxiety, which reinforces your original sense that they are unsafe and best to be avoided. Or consider the complaint of an exhausted mother who says, "My child is so incompetent and helpless! I must shield him from harm, prevent him from endangering himself, anticipate any risk!" This very course of action, designed to cope with a helpless and incompetent child, is an excellent way to *produce* a helpless and incompetent child!

Let's take a longer look at another example drawn from the work of Watzlawick, Weakland and Fisch, psychotherapists who have made a special study of problem-resolution. A pair of overhelpful parents, wanting only the best for their son and his wife, keep pressing their financial and practical help on the young couple. The couple find their "help" intrusive, controlling and guilt-inducing. The children try to decline their overly-generous offers, or at least return the favors to even things up. But the parents won't back off. Indeed, the more the young couple protests their continuing help, the more the parents press it on them.

Why is the system self-sealing? Perhaps the parents find the protests of the young couple rewarding—an affirmation of the genuine extreme helpfulness of their efforts, a confirmation that they are willing to give their all for their children's happiness. Thus the straightforward protesting by the young couple, which is quite a normal and reasonable reaction to stop the parents' unwanted help, only serves to aggravate the problem and to encourage the parents to help out even more.

What can you do to cope with self-sealing systems like this one? The dynamics of self-sealing systems offer a clue: remember, the major characteristic of a self-sealing system is that the very action you take to break the block—however sensible and reasonable that action may be—serves instead to perpetuate it. Therefore, you can sometimes break the seal by doing the *counter*-intuitive, taking an action that may seem quite *contrary* to these sensible and reasonable instincts.

Let's return to the case of the couple and their over-helpful parents. Having tried to fend off the parents in very reasonable ways, with no success at all, the couple was counseled to do the opposite: to accept the parents' offers with an air of entitlement. "By all means, clean the house, Mom; don't forget to sweep the living room." "Sure we'd like a new barbeque; when will you deliver it?" "Yes, let's go out to dinner, your treat."

This sort of response on the part of the couple soon squelched the parents' overzealous helpfulness. They instead turned their parental efforts towards teaching their "overly-dependent" children a lesson in independence by refusing to pamper them and encouraging them to do for themselves—the very result that the children had been quite unable to achieve by more (locally) reasonable means! Morover, after a period of transition, both the couple and the parents were more satisfied with their relationship.

Thus the "locally" intuitive may be the problem; the "locally" counterintuitive may be the solution. This dynamic of self-sealing systems speaks to the importance of thinking in terms of force landscapes. A broader perspective on the contours of the force landscape can help to develop an understanding of, and strategic control over, counterintentional behavior by expanding your view beyond the "local."

Blocked From Change

Matthew has suffered from a bad case of math anxiety for years. He does especially poorly on exams. At first, he didn't know

197

what the problem was—only that he hated math and never did well at it. A helpful counselor in high school gave him more of a perspective. "Look what happens to you when you take a math exam," the counselor pointed out. "You clutch, right?" Matthew nodded. "You can't seem to remember what you know?" Matthew nodded. "You feel stupid?" Matthew nodded again. "No wonder exams make you so anxious!" Through his counselor's good-natured chiding, Matthew recognized the self-defeating pattern that had captured him, in effect a self-sealing system where more anxiety about math promoted "clutching," which led in turn to more anxiety.

Unfortunately, recognizing the problem did little to dispel it. On the strength of his humanities grades, Matthew entered a good college with moderate math and science requirements. Even these gave Matthew a lot of trouble, so he tried again to tackle his entrenched aversion by consulting with a counselor. Would better mathematical problem solving skills help? Matthew learned a few new techniques, but they didn't seem to stick with him when he got anxious during quizzes. How about a desensitization approach? Matthew, with the guidance of a counselor, practiced taking math exams and relaxing. It did help some; Matthew's second-term grades moved from a borderline C − to a safer C + . Still, Matthew and his counselor both felt that he was not doing nearly as well as his general abilities allowed.

What about the deep roots of Matthew's attitude toward math? He traced these back to a particularly difficult experience in the fourth grade with fractions arithmetic, when he felt humiliated in math class by an insensitive teacher. But this review of the past seemed to do little for the problems of the present.

Poor Matthew seems to be more than just blocked. You might say that Matthew is *blocked from change*. Efforts to resolve his problem all seem to come to nothing. Disclosing hidden forces, recognizing a self-sealing system, understanding the roots of his attitude—all these show barely any improvement in Matthew's math anxiety.

In this respect, Matthew resembles many other people blocked into, out of, or between many other behaviors. A reluctant smoker may try a dozen different ways to quit, yet each in turn may leave him as much of a chimney as ever. Employees who continually argue with their bosses may eventually understand their problems better, realize the forces at work, recognize signs of impending loss of temper. And, while some will do better, some still can only count the weeks before they have a real blowup and are looking at want ads again.

So should blocked-from-change be analyzed as a new kind of block, something beyond second-order effects, thrall, primrose paths, and so on? Probably not. Blocked-from-change makes ample sense simply as an extreme case of the familiar patterns we have already dealt with.

Blocked-From-Change As Plain Old Block

Very strong forces. For example, one mechanism of block simply is a strong force—the sort that seems to figure in considerable addictive behavior. How might this apply in Matthew's case? Matthew has been mathphobic for years and years. Each bad experience with math deepens his math terror. It might be that, by this point in Matthew's life, whatever the original sources of the math anxiety, Matthew's aversion to mathematics has become such a strong reflex that it's simply very difficult for Matthew to break the pattern by any means. He may not be dealing merely with strong forces, but with *very* strong forces.

Very self-sealing systems. Another dimension of Matthew's problem was its self-sealing character, where new failures kept reaffirming Matthew's belief that he can't handle mathematics. Well, what if the system is *very* self sealing? What if the efforts of Matthew's counselors become part of the self-sealing process itself? For example, suppose that Matthew thinks not just that he's unable to handle math, but that nothing can help. For whatever reason—his expectation or other factors—the first couple of efforts fail. Matthew's expectation is confirmed and he begins to think of his situation as not just difficult, but hopeless. New interventions with a discouraged Matthew are all the more likely to fail, and, when they do, seal the system tighter. Matthew is caught not merely in a self-sealing system, but in a *very* self-sealing system.

Very subtle hidden forces. Matthew traced his mathphobia to fourth-grade problems with fractions arithmetic. But what if the matter goes much deeper than that? Matthew's father is an engineer with a cool, logical and ironic attitude, as well as high expectations for his family. Perhaps Matthew's commitment to the humanities *and* trouble with math are subtle ways of flouting his father's demands. "My son a poet! Good God!" Or, to bring the therapeutic process into the picture, perhaps Matthew feels lonely away from home and hasn't made many new friends. His contact with a college counselor is one of his few deep relationships, and he is reluctant to "get well" too quickly and loose this intimacy. Thus, Matthew's mathphobia may be influenced not merely by subtle hidden forces but by *very* subtle hidden forces.

We could go on with other mechanisms of block. But the general point should be clear. Mechanisms of block already discussed offer plenty of ways to explain the stubbornness of Matthew's trouble. The question is, what to do then?

How Blocked-From-Change Changes Our Picture
of the Problem

While blocked-from-change involves no fundamentally new and different mechanisms of block, it still makes a difference in our picture of the landscape. When you find yourself blocked-from-change, if nothing else, it's a signal to think more profoundly about the landscape of forces underlying the difficulty. You might search more vigilantly for hidden forces, scan more widely to detect the outer edges of a self-sealing system, review a longer span of time to catch sight of a primrose path, consider the multiple levels of the cycle of causation to discern second-order effects, and so on. Broadly speaking, although one very strong force may be the culprit, it's more likely that blocked-from-change involves a variety of factors at many levels, all over the force landscape.

For these very reasons, the phenomenon of blocked-from-change testifies to the importance of professional help. To be sure, people can often make some progress in block-busting through individual action. In a statistical sense, most blocks probably yield this way. Conversations with close friends, honest self-scrutiny, and even books like this one may help reflective people to help themselves. But blocked-from-change warns that the problem may be subtle or deeply rooted. The blocked person, being part of the force landscape, is likely to be much less able to see it clearly, especially since some of the forces in action may work *against* seeing it clearly. A new and more objective perspective on the situation is one important contribution of the professional counselor.

Blocked-from-change also may signal the need to accept the problem in question. Perhaps Matthew's math anxiety simply is not going to improve dramatically; too many factors sustain his feelings and behavior. He and those helping him need to consider other tacks—minimizing the effect on his grade-point average, moderating Matthew's expectations so that he feels relieved rather than unhappy about C + 's, bolstering Matthew's general self-esteem by, for example, forming a support group with other generally able but mathphobic students. Living comfortably with the problem becomes the goal rather than eliminating the problem. All this might even alleviate Matthew's math anxiety, at least to the extent that it relieves the second-order effects.

Perhaps, also, Matthew should be supported in those activities or pursuits he is *good* at and *happy* doing. Matthew may need to recognize that he can choose *not* to fulfill all of his father's expectations for him, especially if those expectations don't match Matthew's own strengths. For many cases of severe block, it's smart to rethink expectations—not so that you settle for second-best, but rather so that you do what's really best for *you*.

There is an important corollary: being blocked-from-change does *not* necessarily signal any profound psychological pathology. To be sure, when you have repeatedly tried without success to break a stubborn block, it's only natural, although very distressing to wonder, ''Is there something seriously wrong with me?'' And, to be sure, people who are profoundly psychologically disturbed often are blocked-from-change. But the converse simply does not hold: Being blocked-from-change does not imply that you are profoundly disturbed.

Indeed, nothing could be more commonplace than blocked-from-change. People fail to quit smoking after many efforts, fall of their diets and regain the ten pounds they lost, carry on in family squabbles for years, struggle to wake up on Saturday in time for a full and fruitful day only to sleep in until noon—and still live generally normal and rewarding lives. Unwelcome though blocked-from-change may be, we at least can avoid the negative second-order effect of feeling that it means something is drastically wrong with us. If anything, it marks our rueful participation in an all too human condition.

ThinkAbouts

What does all this mean to you? How might you continue to think about the ideas presented in this chapter?

• Real life blocks rarely reflect the influence of just one or two simple forces. Especially when you aren't merely blocked, you are blocked between alternative courses of action, or you are getting into the same block over and over, or you are blocked from change.

• If you find yourself blocked between alternative courses of action, it may help to get more information, to mentally carry out each option in its logical endpoint (that is, try it on for size) or to create or synthesize new options.

• If you find yourself repeating history—getting into the same block over and over—you're probably reacting in any given moment only to the most immediate influences, losing sight of the bigger picture. Try to locate your short-term behavior in a larger pattern of forces.

• If you find yourself blocked from change, maybe the forces influencing your behavior are stronger, more subtle, or less obvious than you thought. It might be helpful to seek professional help in your efforts to understand the complexities of your particular situation. You may even find that other ways of making sense of your behavior—other theories besides force theory—are more useful for you.

Part III

A BROADER VIEW

The five mechanisms of block—strong forces, hidden forces, second-order effects, thralls and landscapes—form a theory of counterintentional behavior. Like all theories, this one has its strengths and weaknesses. Reviewing the theory and thinking critically about it will help you determine how it applies to your own particular situation.

Chapter 8

FORCE THEORY CONCENTRATE

Introduction

In this chapter and the next, we stand back from "force theory" and ponder what it is, how it works, and what it means. Force theory, like any theory, has its own special utility and peculiar limits, both worth examining. This chapter reviews force theory as we have so far developed it, and the next chapter considers the theory more comparatively, critically and philosophically.

Let's begin with a very basic question: What is force theory, anyway? Is it even a real theory, with a capital T? Or merely an appealing metaphor?

Certainly the notions of "force" and "block," so central to the theory, are metaphors. And one might dismiss force theory as "merely" metaphoric, on the assumption that the "hard" sciences of "real" reality are somehow *not* metaphoric. On the contrary, even the rigorously developed notion of "force" in the field of physics is metaphorically derived—from our kinesthetic sense of what we feel or exert when we push or pull on something. The word "force" (from the Latin, *fortis*, meaning strong) has been around since long before the field of modern physics, but because it has served us so well in physics, the concept has lost much of its metaphoric status and we think of physical forces (like gravity) as being "real" rather than metaphoric. In effect, what we consider "real" reality probably has more to do with how well our theories or conceptions work than with whether they are metaphoric or not.

Indeed, dropping metaphor from our language is an effort to be more "scientific" or more "real" is quite impossible. A philosopher colleague of ours once illustrated the point nicely in a story about a fastidious fellow scholar, who spoke out about the dangers of metaphor obscuring ideas. This scholar summed up his concern by announcing, "And I'm busy expunging from my speech all uses of metaphor at any level!"

"*Level?*" our keen friend inquired. "*Expunge?*"

Furthermore, to say that force theory is "merely a metaphor" gives short shrift to the power of metaphor, which plays a crucial role in our efforts to describe our existentially private and isolated internal experiences. Metaphors can be wonderfully evocative, raising in us instant feelings of recognition (when they seem to fit our experience) or rejection and differentiation (when they do not seem to fit our experience). Either reaction is a helpful step in better understanding ourselves and communicating with one another about our experiences.

So force theory is not "merely" metaphoric but a "real" theory in its own right. It represents a systematized description of certain human experiences and behaviors. It defines common or unifying principles that underly disperate phenomena. Its validity is grounded in clinical example and practice as well as everyday experience. That is, force theory broadly meets some basic requirements for theory-hood.

208

Force Theory Concentrate

How Block Happens

The next question is: What does force theory say about block? Block, or more formally counterintentional behavior, has been our central focus since the first pages of this book. Day in and day out, in innumerable ways, people find themselves behaving contrary to their own best intentions. So counterintentional behavior makes a natural focus for any inquiry into the workings of human motivation and intention. And force theory, as a theory of human behavior, should inform our understanding of how block happens. From what mechanism, what slipping of gears, what rousing of demons, what upwelling of pressures, does block arise?

Mechanisms of Block

A central message of force theory is that block is anything but a monolithic phenomenon. Block does not happen for one reason, but for different reasons on different occasions and often for many reasons on the same occasion.

Psychological forces. In our everyday language and culture lies a simple idea about what makes us do what we do: psychological forces. These forces spur us on or hold us back. Anything that can be construed as a vector, with direction and magnitude, qualifies as a force—including the human will, the seat of our intentionality. Block occurs when other psychological forces interfere with our force of will.

The first chapter of the book describes this Everyday Force Theory, and every chapter since has introduced a different way in which forces cause counterintentional behavior. Here are the main ones:

Strong forces. Blocks are often remarkably stubborn simply because the forces are very strong. Strong forces come from many sources. For instance, several weaker forces that happen to "point in the same direction" can add up to a very strong force. Forces associated with primary drives, such as the drive to survive, typically carry great strength.

When counterintentional behavior threatens, we often try to pit our will power against other forces. Indeed, the very term *will power* shows that we think of the will as a pretty hefty psychological force. Unfortunately, the other forces often win out. Will power on the whole is not as strong a force as we like to think.

Hidden forces. The forces producing our counterintentional behavior are not always easy to spot. They can lurk out of sight. They can shape our behavior and, in particular, lead to blocks of various sorts without our being readily able to identify them.

Hidden forces can be just as strong as any others. But, when they work against our best intentions, they are insidious as well. Because we cannot recognize them easily, they are more difficult to deal with.

Second-order forces. Forces arise not only as we react to things in the world, but also as we react to ourselves. You may feel ashamed of your anger, angry at your shame, nervous about being nervous, and so on. Such second-order forces can be real troublemakers. Take for instance, your fear of being afraid. If it were not for the extra factor of *fear*-of-fear, you could perhaps cope with the original fear itself.

Thrall. There's another curious side to block called "thrall." This is a handy name for a phenomenon all too easy to find in our own lives: It's often harder to get out of something once you have started than to refrain in the first place. In other words, the grip of an activity can exceed its pull. We see such thrall effects in

210

everyday binges and in addictive behavior—like gorging on potato chips or smoking cigarettes.

Landscape effects. As if strong forces, hidden forces, second-order effects and thrall were not enough, yet another mechanism figures into block. Blocks can result from a "landscape" effect—the operation of a system of forces coming from more than just one place. For example, a person may get blocked between two different but equally enticing job offers. Or someone may follow again and again the same circular path of behavior, with the forces at each step nudging the person just one step further until ultimately the whole pattern repeats. Or you may find yourself caught up in self-sealing systems where seemingly reasonable efforts to break out actually strengthen the block. Escalating military and political actions are large scale examples, but the same things happen often in everyday life, such as when your efforts to placate an angry lover only make things worse.

How Mysteries Point to Mechanisms

Strong forces, hidden forces, second-order effects, thrall and landscape effects are five kinds of mechanisms that go far toward explaining the various blocks we face in our lives. Moreover, they go well beyond the nature of forces as recognized in our everyday culture and vocabulary, "everyday force theory." But where do these ideas come from? Why do we need them at all? What's wrong with the more basic Everyday Force Theory?

In an historical sense, the "where do they come from?" question has a straightforward answer. Most of the concepts discussed here have been developed by psychologists and therapists concerned with block and other psychological problems that people encounter. Though we've used our own language, most of

211

the ideas synthesized here have precedents in one school of psychology or another.

Psychologists and clinicians have invented these ideas to understand and explain block better. Each one of these ideas goes beyond Everyday Force Theory in order to illuminate what otherwise would be a mystery.

For example, looking at how people behave, we can see that they are forever trying to solve problems of block with pure will power—and failing. Why? Everyday Force Theory tends to view the will as a strong force that occasionally falters, but this leaves a mysterious puzzle: if the will is so strong, why does will power so often fail? Force theory addresses this mystery by proposing that the will is a generally weak force, that the other forces are often stronger than we think, and that a strategic application of the will serves better than a "try harder" approach that mistakenly relies on raw will power.

We are mystified by other aspects of human behavior that Everyday Force Theory doesn't explain. Why does a father snap at his son when his son hasn't done anything to deserve it? Why is a student failing at school despite her considerable academic abilities and no obvious distractions? The operation of strong, obvious forces doesn't go far in explaining these blocks. But we can add the notion of hidden forces to make sense of this otherwise mysterious behavior.

In the same vein, the mystery of why people make mountains out of molehills suggests the notion of second-order effects. The mystery of why people binge leads to the idea of thrall. The mystery of how people get stuck in repetitive-patterns points to the notion of landscape effects. Step by step, the puzzles of why people behave as they do lead us to a richer and more powerful force theory.

How the Mechanisms Are Adaptive

So all these force mechanisms can give us explanations for mysterious cases of block. But that in itself opens up another mystery: how could we possibly live with so many different ways of behaving counterintentionally? It seems inconceivable that nature could have saddled us with such difficulties.

The answer is that these mechanisms are not usually troublemakers—they normally benefit us. What good does it do us, for example, to be so easily controlled by strong forces? It is vital that certain forces like sexuality and hunger be strong to ensure species and individual survival. Why is it adaptive that forces can be hidden? Because the capacity of the human mind to keep track of many things at once is quite limited, and our ability to attend to information selectively, while the rest remains "hidden" from us, prevents us from being flooded by disorganized perceptions and ideas.

Second-order forces serve adaptive purposes, too. Although self-consciousness can be painful sometimes, second-order effects allow you to perceive yourself, reflect on what you see, and act on those reflections—capacities essential to learning, creativity and effective problem-solving. The "grip-is-greater-than-pull" mechanism of thrall ensures that we will be orderly and productive in our behavior, rather than flighty and distractable. While it sometimes locks us into one thing too strongly, it's crucial in organizing our behavior.

In landscape effects, it's certainly awkward to be "blocked between" a number of different forces. On the other hand, when you have more than one option, it's generally a good idea to pause and reflect about which way to, rather than heading off impulsively in one direction or another. Likewise, it's certainly

213

unfortunate to be led down primrose paths. But traveling in response to local forces is often a perfectly sensible way to navigate through a complex world; only a few paths lead to danger. And so on.

The basically adaptive nature of the mechanisms that underlie block is worth bearing in mind, both for the sake of an objective picture and for the sake of feeling reasonably good about ourselves. Counterintentional behavior is troublesome enough without the thought that it reflects something deeply wrong with the structure of our minds. On the contrary, counterintentional behavior is an occasional unfortunate side effect of mechanisms that most of the time serve us well.

Ways of Change

Another important theme throughout these pages has been how change happens. How can people go over, under, around or through blocks, or simply learn to live more comfortably with them? Though the answer is as complex as the mechanisms of block (and the mechanisms are diverse indeed), it's possible to chart in a broad way how change can occur.

The Circle of Causation and Its Levels

A useful organizer for both explaining block and charting ways of change is the "circle of causation." This circle helps us to map the multiple mechanisms of behavior by drawing our attention to four loci:

- Encounter with the world
- Perception of what's encountered
- Forces evoked by perceptions
- Response shaped by forces

A person's response generates another immediate encounter with the world, and so the circle continues.

The circle is especially handy for thinking about block, because a pattern of counterintentional behavior—like any pattern of behavior—necessarily depends on all points in the cycle. Consequently, any point in the circle is a place to interrupt and divert it into more constructive paths.

A helpful extension to the circle of causation recognizes multiple levels of the cycle:

The first-order circle. This circle concerns the world as we normally experience it. We encounter the world, we perceive it, forces are evoked in response, and we act within and upon the world as the forces move us.

The second-order circle. We human beings often pay attention to ourselves as well as to the world beyond ourselves. We encounter ourselves—hearing ourselves speak, seeing ourselves in mirrors, confronting our thoughts. We thus perceive ourselves, which evokes forces and in turn yields responses. This "second-order circle" is crucial to recognize, since many times counterintentional behavior involves reactions to oneself rather than or in addition to one's situation in the world.

The third-order circle. Here, the self encounters and perceives the self's perceptions of the self. Confusing though that sounds, it means something fairly straightforward: third-order thinking allows us, for example, to identify and change our problematic self-images. Pulling back to such a distanced perspective affords us this added understanding and leverage.

215

Some Ways of Change

All this offers a neat overall organization, but the potential for change lies specifically in the way that an event plays out at each point of the circle.

Encounter. When you change your encounter with the world, your counterintentional behavior may disappear even though everything else about you remains the same. That is, if you encounter the original situation again, you will perceive it in the old way, the usual forces will be evoked, and the counterintentional behavior will reappear. Whereas your "inner person" has not changed at all, a different encounter with the world has nevertheless remade your behavior.

For example, people can modify their encounters with the world by changing their environment, as Enoch did by storing cookies out of sight. People also can modify their encounters by traveling differently through their world, as Emma, for instance, avoided the liquor store on her way home from work. When several people are involved in a self-sealing system, an alteration in one person's behavior can change the world all the others encounter, thus breaking down the whole system.

Regarding the second-order cycle, people can encourage reflective encounters with themselves simply by setting aside time to mull over their circumstances, talk things over with a friend, or consult with a therapist. Most therapists take special pains to make a therapeutic session an occasion for reflection. Such occasions often involve a third-order circle, as you see yourself trapped by certain second-order cycles and find ways to redirect them.

Perception. In cases of perceptual change, you encounter the same old world, but you see it differently. Because of your new

216

perceptions, new forces are evoked and new reactions follow, altering the pattern of counterintentional behavior that was originally troubling you. Although many things can change perceptions, insight is perhaps the most available resource: you remake your perception of the world and of yourself by understanding things differently.

For example, cigarettes can come to look less sophisticated, more dangerous. Loud words from a boss can come to sound less sadistic, more frustrated. Situations may get "reframed" into very different guises: a problem becomes an opportunity, a mild risk an adventure. All this may also happen on the level of the second-order circle, especially with the help of third-order reflection. You may, for instance, reclassify personal traits as owned rather than unowned, or unowned rather than owned, changing your attitude about yourself.

Forces. When there's a change in evoked forces, the world a person encounters remains essentially the same, perceptions follow as before, but different forces are aroused. How can this happen?

Certain kinds of experiences can "remap" the connection between perceptions and forces. Conditioning, for example, can create a link between perceptions and forces that did not exist before: A close call with a snarling dog—or even a sufficiently vivid story about it—can lead a child to be wary of a loving pet. Likewise, deconditioning can break undesirable links, as when a person with a phobia practices relaxation techniques in the face of the feared object.

Response. Even when you encounter the same world as usual, perceive it in the same way, and find the same forces evoked, you can change your patterns of reaction to avoid counterintentional behavior. A hot-tempered man might learn to react with a soft

217

firm voice, an alternative way of expressing anger that is less likely to escalate the conflict.

In cases when you are "blocked in" to an undesirable behavior pattern, anything that postpones your usual response can be a powerful remedy. Recall that Rhea used the tactic of counting to twenty before giving her temper its head; by the time she finished the count, her fury had faded. In cases when you are "blocked out" of doing something, a symbolic gesture towards it sometimes helps you get fully into it, as when you drag yourself out of bed in the morning by starting with the twitch of a toe.

It seems nonsensical to suggest that a different response can follow, when all the original forces are the same. Actually, it's more accurate to say that the *major* forces are the same. When, for instance, you count to ten to quell your anger, your anger is still the strongest force at large. But your relatively weak will is another force, which, though it cannot suppress the anger directly, *can* get you to count, which in turn diffuses the anger. Likewise, when you substitute a low, firm voice for a louder one, your angry response is not so much quelled as diverted. Trying to speak softly does nothing to change the original force and thus your anger; still, it introduces a new, small force, directing your attention towards minding what you are saying rather than pouring full force into venting your rage.

When Things Get Better, What Changes?

We usually think that psychological change is a change in the *self*. We have somehow become fundamentally different and can now cope better with circumstances that previously seemed too painful to bear. However, such a belief considerably oversimplifies things. Why? Because the forces that you experience and that determine your behavior are not just a matter of who you are and what your psychological makeup is, but also a matter of where you stand in a larger system of external events and other people. How you behave depends in large part on how other things and other people in the larger system behave.

To put this in terms of the circle of causation, one might say that behavior emerges from nested, layered, interlocking and simultaneously occurring circles, some of which are yours and some other people's. Where change occurs, in what circle, and at what level, and in what combinations, can vary widely.

Take a self-sealing system example from the last chapter, for instance. Are the parents and the young couple fundamentally different psychologically after the painful behavior pattern has been broken? Not necessarily. Yet they are all much happier and less blocked. Their pattern of interaction had a life of its own, and *that* is what has changed.

So when things get better, what changes? The circle of causation offers many answers. Perhaps it's what you encounter that changes: you keep cigarettes out of the house, although you sure would like one. Or it's what you perceive: you've reframed your cigarette habit as infantile and that helps you hold back. Or it's how you respond: you've managed to form the habit of counting to ten before replying when someone offers you a cigarette, making it easier for you to say no. Or perhaps after you've been off cigarettes for a while, the forces themselves change: you no longer feel the *urge* to smoke when you see a cigarette. Or, at the level of a second-order circle, it's what you think of yourself: you used to think of yourself as helpless and not responsible for your smoking but now you "own" the behavior. Or, concerning landscapes: perhaps you find it easier to quit since your wife quit with you, and since your kids have begun to pester you about cigarette smoke in the house. And so on.

One could spin out the tale of possibilities at greater length, of course, but the point is clear. It's limiting to think of change as a matter of necessarily changing the self, and particularly limiting to think of change as necessarily involving change in how the self feels about things (such as whether or not you badly want a cigarette). Rather, change can happen in many ways at many levels.

When Change Won't Happen

The many resources for change afforded by the four points on the circle of causation by no means guarantee an easy solution to counterintentional behavior. There are plenty of ways that any plan for change can go wrong. Enoch may well put the cookies out of sight, changing his environment. But it may be hard to *keep* them out of sight. Suppose he takes them out once. Does he remember to put them back in the cupboard again? He might forget because it's easy to forget, or because he doesn't *really* want to deprive himself of cookies. Or the kids could forget to put them away. So sooner or later Enoch encounters them again on the kitchen counter and he's back where he started. Or Penny may well reject her therapist's suggestion, a new way to perceive study time. Forrest, who joined AA, may find that the group isn't a strong enough new force to fight against his addiction. And Rhea, after changing her reactions by counting to ten, may turn around only to hear yet another idiotic comment, and feel her rage welling up all over again.

In general, despite the many resources for change, a block can easily snap back into place. Not because the mind is perverse; often circumstances are to be blamed. The habits of others, the inevitabilities of the environment, and so on, continue to exert their forces upon you. A persistent block would not have arisen in the first place if there weren't enough going to keep it there, so it is understandable that circumstances are likely to restore the pattern even as you try to change it.

Change is not easy or inevitable. Still, none of this is reason to despair. In fact, in most situations, there is potential for real and productive change. So when change won't happen despite your best efforts, and you are getting tired and discouraged, don't give up—ask for help.

A Theory Among Theories

After this strong dose of force theory concentrate, the next chapter has a very different focus. Rather than speaking through the mouth and seeing through the eyes of force theory, as we did in this chapter, we will try to disengage ourselves from the theory and assess it from the outside. Force theory is a way of looking at and understanding the world, but far from the *only* way. So assessing force theory requires placing it in context, examining it in comparison and in contrast with other psychological perspectives on human motivation, and on block in particular. We must come to some sense of force theory as one meaning-world among many in the larger universe of therapeutic practices and theories, cultural understandings and contexts. Only in this way can we fruitfully ask what its assumptions are, where its strengths and weaknesses lie, and what is the nature and extent of its usefulness.

ThinkAbouts

What does all this mean to you*? How might you continue to think about the ideas presented in this chapter?*

• With a little practice, you can learn to identify the strong forces, the hidden forces, the second-order forces, and thralls and the landscape effects that account for your counterintentional behavior.

• These five ways of explaining block share two characteristics. First, each responds to some puzzling aspect of block not explained by our more everyday ways of making sense of our behavior. Second, each is grounded in basically good and adaptive mechanisms of human behavior.

• The circle of causation gives you a useful model for charting the dynamics of your behavior. Ask yourself what you *encounter* in the world, what you *perceive* as a result, what *forces* get aroused by your perceptions, and how you are *responding* to these forces. Each point in the circle provides a locus for creative intervention to interrupt the pattern of counterintentional behavior. Nested circles of causation provide models of second-order and third-order effects, too.

Chapter 9

ANALYSIS, POETRY, AND THE MIND'S REALITY

How Do You Size Up a Theory?

Force theory gives us some insight into and leverage over blocks. Great! But really, how *good* a theory is it? After all, there are lots of theories about human behavior and human hangups. There's psychodynamic theory, behavior therapy, existential psychology. There's transactional analysis, transcendental meditation and primal screaming. What makes force theory unique?

We'll tackle this question by taking not one but two close looks at force theory: from the "analytic" side and the "poetic" side.

Now what does that mean? A comment attributed to Albert Einstein captures something of the distinction between the analytic and the poetic; he is said to have remarked that, "A chemical analysis of a cup of soup shouldn't be expected to taste like the soup." His point, of course, is that a technical analysis of something is altogether different from our experience of the thing. Furthermore, we shouldn't mistake one for the other.

It's certainly an easy mistake to make, since a chemical analysis and a taste test *do* both concern the same thing—the cup of soup. Still, they are two entirely different takes on the soup, and you may value them quite differently depending on your purpose. If, on the one hand, you're just wondering whether to order the soup for lunch, you may appreciate knowing the results of a taste test. If, on the other hand, you're on a strict no-salt diet or you're allergic to MSG, you may find the chemical analysis more helpful. Neither approach is more "correct" than the other; rather, they each address something important and they each succeed in ways that the other fails.

When it comes to psychological theories, a similar distinction proves useful. Any theory offers us a tool for technical analysis— its analytic side. And any theory, through its language, imagery and spirit, gives us a vehicle for experiencing the world and ourselves—its poetic side. As with Einstein's soup, the analytic value of a theory and its poetic value shouldn't be confused with one another. But they both should be looked at. Let's see why.

The analytic side of theories. Any theory strives to be technically useful. It tries to offer an accurate description or explanation of certain phenomena and some tools for analyzing them further. Indeed, this is the point of a theory, whether a theory of quantum dynamics or a theory of supply and demand.

Force theory is no different. All the concepts that make up Everyday Force Theory plus the many more we've added in the book—forces, the circle of causation, second-order effects, thrall, and so on—give us an elaborate tool kit for explaining, and sometimes remedying, particular cases of block. This work of rationally explaining and prescribing is what we mean by the analytic side of a theory.

The poetic side of theories. Whatever analytic powers a theory may hold, it also has a kind of poetry to it, a music of

expression, a particular taste. The poetry of a theory is determined largely by its language and guiding imagery. The poetry of
force theory for example, highlights the qualities of force, movement and power. Consider a term like *thrall*, with its connota-
tions of powerlessness or bondage. Or consider a notion like *the
strategic use of the will*, with its almost military intimations.
These contribute to the particular feel of force theory quite
independently of the theory's analytic utility.

Any theory can be assessed in terms of these two sides, and
each is important. That is, it's worth talking both about how a
theory *works* and how it *feels*. It's worth noting both how analytically *consonant* a theory is with the data it hopes to explain and
how poetically *resonant* the theory is with our internal experience
of the world and of ourselves.

What about truth? All this talk about the analytic and poetic
powers of a theory like force theory may seem to miss the point.
What about *truth?* Shouldn't we simply be asking if force theory
is true, or what parts of it are true? Why all this gibberish about
the analytic and poetic sides of a theory?

There is a problem with this line of thought. The question,
"What about truth?" is based on the assumption that we can
measure a theory—determine its rightness or wrongness, its
correctness or incorrectness—against the yardstick of absolute,
constant, true reality, which exists independently of our efforts to
make sense of it. A theory either measures up to this absolute
reality—meaning the theory is true—or fails to measure up—
meaning it is false. At least, one would think, you can measure
the analytic side of a theory this way, and chalk up the poetic side
of a theory as so much window dressing.

The trouble with this assumption is that the truth of a theory is
a much more slippery matter than first appears. Even an *accurate*

225

chemical analysis of a cup of soup, for example, is not really "true" in an absolute sense. It reflects the particular equipment and procedures used to produce it. It reflects the particular level of analysis undertaken—chemical rather than nuclear for example. More sophisticated equipment or a different analytical window will yield a different analysis.

Psychological theories, even analytically strong ones, are similarly context-bound in this way. For example, while proponents of Freudian psychodynamic theory claim that that theory is a technically strong one, some critics suggest it is perhaps only *contextually* strong—specially tuned to the nature of the bourgeois class of 19th century Vienna, where Freud developed it. So the seemingly objective analytic side of a theory is a product of such determining factors as what data was considered, how it was investigated, and who coined the theory.

And what about the notion that the poetic side of a theory is irrelevant to its truth—that poetry is a nicety, a luxury, a matter of aesthetics rather than accuracy? Far from it. The poetry of a theory is crucially important even for theories in the hard sciences that would seem to have few human dimensions. Einstein himself, among many notable scientists and mathematicians, was notorious for his vigorous pursuit of a theory with a powerful poetry—a theory that displayed true elegance, beauty and symmetry. Such characteristics are not only pretty, but practical. They foster simpler, tighter theories that are more likely to disclose fundamental consistencies in the universe.

And poetry seems especially important in the context of clinical psychological theories, where the object of our theorizing is *us*, our own personal life situations. In this context, we look to a theory not only to provide a sound scientific account of human behavior, but also to leave us feeling better understood and better

226

able to understand the experience of others. We expect a theory to respectfully and empathically reflect our inner felt experience. We want to recognize ourselves in it. An intuitively appealing poetry for talking and thinking about human problems—the sort of poetry that will inspire and illuminate—is at a premium in the domain of psychological theories.

So the analytic side of a theory has less to do with truth than you might think, and the poetic side more. They both contribute. And, in the process, the question of *truth* takes on a constructivist cast. When we ask about the analytic and poetic sides of a theory we *are* asking about its truth.

Constructivism suggests that human beings have no way of knowing "real reality." We can only make up theories, models, frameworks, and so on, and see how they play. Do they account for the data so far? Do they predict new data? Do they paint a parsimonious picture of their topics? Do they serve well as tools for controlling our environments and indeed ourselves? In sum, do they *fit* the world as we encounter it and strive to predict and influence it? That's the best we can do as a standard of truth. And that standard involves considerations both analytic and poetic.

So let's roll up our sleeves and see what can be said about the strengths and limitations—analytic and poetic—of force theory.

Force Theory: The Analytic Side

Exploring the analytic side of force theory means evaluating its technical utility. With this goal in mind, let's look at force theory's subject matter, its language, the limits of what the theory covers, its relationship to other theories, and the general advantages and disadvantages of force theory.

227

What Is the Subject Matter of Force Theory?

The most basic characteristic of any theory is its subject matter, what it is about. Quantum electrodynamic theory is about the interaction of light and matter. Economic theory treats the factors that cause prices to fluctuate, trade to flourish or languish, and so on. So what is force theory about?

Force theory aims to explain human motivations and human behavior. As we've developed force theory here, the focus falls on counterintentional behavior in everyday life—block. Although many broad psychological theories have something to say about block, force theory makes a special study of it.

Block is a reasonable, even fortuitous, subject for theorizing, since it's among the things that upset people most in their day-to-day lives. It's not the only thing we find distressful, of course: often external events upset us. But one of the major reasons we get upset with *ourselves* is that we find ourselves behaving contrary to our own intentions. You might even say that block deserves its own theory, rather than receiving incidental or tangential comment from theories focussed elsewhere. Also, block is a roomy concept that assimilates many different sorts of psychological troubles, from difficulty dieting to problems with decision making. For a single concept, it's a remarkably versatile one.

What Is the Language of Force Theory?

One of force theory's most appealing characteristics is its firm grounding in everyday understandings and everyday language. Force theory, remember, was introduced in the early pages of this book as Everyday Force Theory, rooted in the readily recognizable and naturally-occurring terms and concepts that people tend to use in describing and understanding their behavior.

We've expanded and extended these concepts to treat block more deeply and comprehensively. Still, even the specialized language that force theory does employ—blocked in/out, thrall, etc.—is not far so removed from everyday speech. In contrast, terms like "cathexis" from psychodynamic theory or "operant conditioning" from behavior theory seem much further removed from everyday speech and thought.

What Are the Boundaries of Force Theory?

There is a lot that force theory simply doesn't have much to say about. It doesn't much address, for example, seriously patholog-ical behavior like psychoses or major affective disorders. It doesn't have much to say about psychological development from birth to adulthood. And, although it goes far in accommodating individual differences, it pays no special attention to group differ-ences, such as contrasts due to sex, language or culture. Like most theories, force theory as developed here sticks pretty close to its subject matter, counterintentional behavior, and makes few claims about its applicability to other contexts.

Perhaps most importantly, force theory is basically a theory of "normal" rather than "abnormal" behavior. We may not *feel* very normal when we find ourselves overeating, not studying, losing our temper at work. Yet force theory recognizes such shortfalls as a ubiquitous aspect of the human condition. Indeed, force theory specifically declines to consider most counterinten-tional behavior as anything but "normal" behavior. Rather, block is an unfortunate and problematic manifestation of ba-sically normal and indeed adaptive psychological mechanisms.

Think of it this way: Most crazy behavior is counterintentional, but most counterintentional behavior is not crazy.

How Is Force Theory Similar to Other Theories?

Most of force theory's central concepts are far from original. For example, the notion of displacement from Chapter 3 is an important part of psychoanalytic theory. The phenomenon of "second-order effects" has claimed the attention of a number of psychologists. The idea of "self-sealing systems" of attitudes and beliefs is a widespread one, important to several contemporary perspectives.

Perhaps the most important common ground between force theory and other views is the underlying force metaphor itself. Not only our everyday langauge but also many Western psychological perspectives incorporate a physics/force metaphor. They assume, often tacitly, that psychological forces move a person from Point A to Point B; the most powerful force or combination of forces at work determines how the person behaves. As a result of this shared sense of how people function psychologically, such very different perspectives as Freudian psychoanalytic theory and Rogerian self theory can speak of "energy sources" within the individual that direct behavior. Force theory shares these same roots.

Of course, it is no accident that force theory holds its force metaphor and many other notions like displacement in common with other theories: in articulating force theory, we have tried to harvest insightful and useful ideas from many sources. At the same time, the fact that ideas like force and displacement are frequently heard should not be taken as evidence of their ultimate validity.

On the contrary, we'd say that force theory is *bounded* by its particular cultural assumptions. The force metaphor is a peculiarly 19th/20th century Western one—there are other metaphors more popular and meaningful in other cultures, subcultures or times. Many Eastern perspectives, for example, reflect not the power orientation of a force metaphor but a more holistic orientation of what might be called a harmony metaphor. In such a world view, qualities of harmony and balance, rather than of power and motion, govern human behavior. In such a world view, the very term block makes little sense; rather, one might be concerned with issues of disharmony or incongruence. (We'll talk a little more about what might be called "harmony theory" in contrast with force theory later in the chapter.)

How Does Force Theory Differ From Other Theories?

One way force theory contrasts with other contemporary theories is in its focus on block. We've already mentioned this. Of course, the concepts of force, displacement, hidden forces, and so on, are useful in discussing many other situations besides those where block looms large. But, in building force theory as an extension of Everyday Force Theory, we've paid particular attention to counterintentional behavior and highlighted concepts that help in understanding and dealing with counterintentional behavior.

Force theory also contrasts with many contemporary theories in its focus on essentially *normal* human behavior. As we've emphasized over and over, block is commonplace. And it's the side effect of psychological mechanisms that usually function much to our benefit. While force theory does not have a lot to say about really pathological behavior, it has a great deal to say about the psychological barriers of everyday life.

231

Finally, force theory contrasts with many current theories in its chosen level of generality. Force theory tries to find the essence of block and change in quite general principles rather than particular forces or change mechanisms. Take the basic question, "What causes block?" Many theories answer with emphasis on *particular* forces—Oedipal urges, or problems of self-esteem, or particular environmental stimuli. Or some combination. But force theory answers with what *general* configurations of forces cause trouble—powerful forces, second-order effects, thralls, self-sealing systems, etc. Sure, force theory wants to know what specific forces are at work in specific cases. But most any strong force or gang of weaker forces can set up a situation of block. It's not specific forces that make for block but their strength and pattern.

Similarly, many theories of human motivation highlight two or three particular mechanisms of *change* as most important—for one theory, deconditioning may be prominent; for another, developing insights may be most important. In contrast, force theory emphasizes the circle of causation and the variety of change mechanisms available at the different points and levels of the circle—including deconditioning and developing insights, among many others. So force theory describes the formal *structure* of block and change, rather than specifying the *particular* forces or mechanisms that account for given instances of counterintentional behavior.

The Pros and Cons of Eclecticism

Force theory's emphasis on structure over particulars has its pros and cons. One advantage is that force theory, by not adopting any specific list of forces that are "likely culprits" in producing

232

counterintentional behavior, makes us keep our eyes open to the complexities of human situations. Too often, commitment to a particular list of "likely culprit" forces can be blinding. Abraham Maslow is said to have commented, "If all you have in your toolbox is a hammer, you tend to treat everything like a nail." If suppressed libidinal urges are at the top of your force list, then you are likely to see suppressed libidinal urges wherever you look.

In contrast, force theory argues that the operative forces in human behavior and block in particular are enormously diverse. Block typically emerges from the *pattern* of the play of forces—hidden forces, self-sealing, and so on—no matter what the particular forces involved. To understand a situation of block, you need to be alert to the patterns that yield block and search flexibly for the particular forces.

This leads to another advantage of force theory's eclecticism: force theory makes a pretty good common language for comparing different theories. Because force theory doesn't have a force list of its own, it can with studied neutrality talk about the force lists of psychoanalytic therapy or cognitive therapy or behavioral therapy—what they are, how they compare, what mechanisms they posit, and so on. Because almost any causal entity can be constructed as a force, different theories can be brought into dialog using force theory as an interlingua.

However, the eclectic stance of force theory runs a risk as well. What if suppressed libidinal urges—or some other specific and identifiable force—*are* the principal players in block? Well, then it would certainly make sense to have a specific list of "likely culprit" forces featuring suppressed libidinal urges rather than just having a general structure like the one offered by force theory. In other words, if there *is* a short list of "likely culprit" forces, we certainly ought to have it and use it in our efforts to help one another live happier and more intentional lives. Certainly many theories of motivation *claim* that they have the "right" short list and that they have identified the particular forces that "really" cause the trouble. So the risk in force theory's deliberate eclecticism is that it will miss the boat—it downplays the notion of a "correct" force list so strongly that it wouldn't even recognize one should one exist!

Overall, we feel the benefits of force theory's eclectic stance outweigh the risks. We do not see a compelling case for a short list of "likely culprit" forces. Indeed, the diversity of force lists from one theory to the next—never mind from one culture to the next—seems to argue against that.

Force Theory: The Poetic Side

The poetry of a theory stands apart from its analytic utility. The poetry is a matter of how the theory feels, how it resonates with our internal experience. A theory's poetry comes from its language, its assumptions, its guiding metaphor. It can be sensed in how a theory looks and sounds. The poetry of a theory is something like the taste of Einstein's soup.

So is poetry important? After all, it's easy to see the poetry of a theory as a frill, a nonessential and non-functional side of the theory. Maybe force theory's poetry makes no more difference in our effort to understand block than the color of a car makes in our effort to drive to the store. So long as the car runs well, what difference does its color make? So long as the theory yields a good analysis, what difference does its poetry make?

We'll argue that it makes a big difference. So let's get on with evaluating force theory in terms of its poetic imagery, with a close look at what poetry it projects, the inherent biases, the differing effects on different people, and the role of poetry in practical problem solving about block.

What Is Force Theory's Poetry?

Force theory intimates that we often are at the mercy of psychological forces that shape our behavior, much as physical objects are at the mercy of the forces that determine their movement. In order to garner the power to act according to our intentions, we have to use our wits. We have to manage better the forces in our lives.

Sailing the sea of forces, you might say. If we isolate the "up" side of this notion, some images emerge—the triumphant sailor weathering rough seas, the surfer riding a wave. Or, to be less nautical about it, the valiant marathoner crossing the finish line, or the gleeful chess player executing a brilliant checkmate. These capture the sense of the individual in control, master of the forces at work.

On the other hand, if we isolate the "down" side, the poetry speaks of the individual helpless in a sea of swirling forces, like a swimmer caught in the undertow. Or a weary and discouraged soldier fighting a losing battle, or a small screaming child being dragged to the dentist. These images capture the sense of the individual outnumbered or outweighed, helpless or weak, at the mercy of the forces at work.

In other words, the poetry of force theory speaks of power and powerlessness, of control and lack of control, of freedom and constraint. The feel of force theory is an us-against-them, a me-against-the-forces feeling. It smacks of strategy, of conflict, of

235

gaining ground, of winning and losing. Both the upbeat and downbeat aspects of force theory's poetry share a strong orientation towards power issues, with such concepts as strength, leverage, impact and strategy as central.

Making this poetry explicit shows up its idiosyncrasy. Certainly we don't have to see all of human behavior as happening under the sun of power-oriented concepts—force theory simply tends to shine that way. Another theory may shine a different way. A theory with an underlying growth metaphor would emphasize concepts like nurturance and transformation rather than power and movement.

What Cultural Biases Underlie Force Theory?

The poetry of force theory is no accident. Everyday force theory inherits its slant from a social context, a culture with certain leanings. This is, of course, more or less true of all human constructions. The poetry of force theory probably resonates with your particular experience in rough proportion to the extent to which you share its cultural roots.

At least three cultural biases of force theory's poetry deserve underscoring here. First, the poetry's power-orientation reflects generally Western values. The competitive achievement ethic and the notion of individual triumph tend to more integral to Western civilizations, philosophies and religions than to many others. To the extent that these power-oriented notions are embedded in the poetry of force theory, the theory has a Western bias.

A second bias of force theory's poetry is its "masculinity." The theory's power-orientated poetry is more consistent with traditionally or stereotypcially masculine characteristics than feminine ones. Different, less "macho" theories, for example, might emphasize such concepts as cooperation, nurturance, compromise or interdependence.

Third, the poetry of force theory is especially appealing to and applicable in adult/intellectual situations. The theory's emphasis on sense-making, on strategy, and on force-management give it a particular feel as a conceptual tool—a tool that may not fit the small hand of a child or that may bend too easily in rough use. Both its complexity and its assumptions about the individual's cognitive and decision making capacities mark the theory as more suited to insight-oriented adults than to children.

How Does the Poetry Help or Hinder Problem Solving?

So there are the biases. And so what? So what if the poetry of force theory has a Western, masculine, adult/intellectual flavor to it? Does that influence its utility?

You bet. Theories don't do anything by themselves. Individuals use theories as tools to think with. And if you don't *like* a theory, you're less likely to use it, no matter how strong the analytic side of the theory. Some people don't like the feel of Freudian theory. Some people don't like the feel of behavior theory. Force theory may turn others off in the same way. Alternatively, an analytically weak theory may enjoy a certain popularity because of its poetic appeal—Leo Buscaglia's "hug therapy" for example.

Moreover, it's not just a matter of likes and dislikes but ease of use. Your sense of good poetic resonance with a theory is likely to make the theory easier to think with. You feel legitimized in your own internal experience. The theory makes sense, inviting you to think harder, to explore further. A good poetic resonance can sometimes be helpful in this way regardless of the analytic acuity of the theory.

So, with all this in mind, who's likely to find force theory most useful? We might expect that adults with an intellectual bent—more so than children or less intellectually-oriented adults—will feel comfortable with force theory. Likewise, we might expect that traditional Westerners more so than traditional Easterners, and traditional men more so than traditional women, will find resonances between the theory and their experience of life. We are speaking overgenerally here, of course, to make a point; these are expectable trends, not hard lines.

Such trends aside, what about the individual? It's natural that people with different styles of thought and commitments will feel differently about force theory. In this regard, force theory's power-oriented poetry is like a double-edged sword that can cut in two directions.

For example, the idea of the "strategic use of will" may energize those who are attracted by the notion of taking charge of themselves intellectually and "tricking" troublesome forces into doing good, or at least doing less harm. These people might find in the notion of a weak will encouragement to use the will strategically, working through understanding the force landscape and manipulating it in key places to trigger changes. They sense a poetry of possibility and opportunity, a poetry of control, and so find inspiration in the theory.

Others, however, may be put off by strategizing about themselves in this manipulative manner. They don't want to have to *outmaneuver* themselves; they simply want to stop *wanting* to smoke, drink, get angry, whatever. The idea that you have to be strategic may not sit well with them at all—it may even seem to them to be inherently compromising. One shouldn't settle for

238

acting differently when what one really wants is to *become* different. These people could easily feel disempowered by force theory's idea of the weak will. They sense a poetry of determinism, a poetry of helplessness, and so find the theory discouraging instead of inspiring. It is ironic that force theory's poetry can undermine the very thing that we all as theory-users and theory-builders hope to foster—greater insight into and control over our counterintentional behavior. Still, the theory may leave some feeling less in command of themselves rather than more so, less in touch with themselves rather than more so.

So What Should I Do If I Don't Like— or Do Like—the Poetry?

Poetry is important. Very important. But for all that, this talk of poetry should not narrow our choices unduly for using force theory or any other theory.

Maybe you don't like the poetry, but it seems to fit your boss to a T; so you think in terms of force theory in your efforts to understand your boss's behavior and to get along with her better. Maybe you like the poetry of force theory, and find that it echoes perfectly your inner experiences, but you decide to keep your thoughts to yourself because you know your friends just aren't as interested in things psychological as you are. Or maybe you're a thoughtful explorer of your own nature: you look at yourself through the window of force theory whether you like the poetry or not, just to see what you see. And you have other windows too.

In other words, just because you don't like the poetry doesn't mean that force theory will never be useful to you; and just because you do like the poetry doesn't mean that force theory will

239

always be the best choice. Life is too complex for such undiscriminating reactions. How well force theory's poetry appeals to you is something to take into account. But not to be dogmatic about.

Alternative Metaphors, Alternative Destinies

Psychological theories tend to speak in metaphors of destiny. Whence have we come? What will we do? Where will we go? How do we get there? Is our path determined or do we choose it?

Force theory answers these questions in terms of the play of forces within and upon us. Force theory tells a tale of destiny something like this: the forces that operate within and upon us determine our destiny, unless we take charge and manage them strategically. The forces often do fine without our meddling. But we can get stuck in painful configurations of forces—block. To avoid block or get out of block, we have to take charge.

We've emphasized throughout this chapter that people can speak in many idioms about why they do as they do. So let's strike a contrast with force theory and consider "harmony theory," another appealing and helpful idiom. Harmony theory is based on what might be called a harmony metaphor rather than a force metaphor. Whereas force theory speaks in the language of psychological forces, stress, conflict, gangs of forces, and so on, harmony theory speaks in the language of psychological harmonies, dissonance, consonance, volume, balance, orchestrations, etc. Whereas force talk says that people respond to the net play of forces, harmony talk says that people seek the most harmonious disposition of factors. And how do you speak in this new idiom? You might say, "Jack is struggling with dissonant internal voices," rather than "Jack is full of internal conflict." You might ask, "What harmony is Jill seeking, or what disharmony is she trying to correct, with her compulsive eating?" rather than "What forces are compelling Jill to eat compulsively?"

In fact—and this is the real kicker—force theory and harmony theory are virtually the same theory from an *analytic* standpoint. It's easy to translate roughly from one to the other. Forces are equivalent to tones or notes. Configurations of forces are equivalent to chords or patterns of harmony and disharmony. Stress or tension is equivalent to dissonance or imbalance. Block is a chronic or continuing disharmony.

Analytically more or less the same. But what a difference! Harmony theory evokes a very different poetry—a poetry that is more Eastern in tone, less stereotypcially masculine. It is a poetry that values beauty and belonging over power and winning.

Juxtaposing the force and harmony idioms provokes us to think yet again about just what theories are and what they do for us. Here we have two theories, one very common in our culture, the other present but rarer. Analytically much the same, poetically quite a contrast. And each has a claim on our allegiance.

What matters is not which one is "right." What matters is our efforts to make sense of things in ways that help us understand them and change them, in this case our efforts to understand and influence counterintentional behavior. So what's "right" is a matter of what *works*; what helps us make sense and effect change. And if two very different idioms do that job on different occasions, or in different ways on the same occasion, or for different people, well, all this in itself is worth noting and incorporating into our ongoing sense-making efforts. And when we long instead for easy answers or quick solutions, we should remind ourselves that the universe is not such a simple place. Especially not that corner of the universe where we quirky human beings abide.

241

ThinkAbouts

What does all this mean to you? How might you continue to think about the ideas presented in this chapter?

• Theories should be treated as the human constructions they are, rather than as absolute truths. Think critically about the theories you encounter, including force theory.

• Look at both the analytic and poetic side of a theory. The analytic side concerns its technical merit—how accurate, useful and complete it is. The poetic side concerns its feel—how it moves us or inspires us, how we resonate to it. Both are important.

• In assessing the virtues and limits of a theory, try to take into account the context out of which the theory arose. All theories are to some extent context-bound: they are rooted in their particular time and place and culture.

• Recognizing theories as human constructions may be disillusioning—it implies that "reality" may not be as certain or as knowable as you'd hoped. But it is inspiring as well—it means that we are the makers of our own understandings. So feel free to revise force theory—and other theories—to help you to make sense of yourself and behave according to your best intentions.

EPILOGUE

A number of years ago, an officer in the army became fascinated by a curious characteristic of the procedure of firing an artillary piece. These large guns are handled by teams, of course. The oddity was that two members of the team would, according to the strictly defined procedure, simply stand some distance to the left rear while the gun was fired. What were they supposed to be doing?

The officer in question began to probe the historical records, tracing back from decade to decade and generation to generation the origins of this feature of the firing procedure. And finally he found it. The two were there to hold the horses.

This tale of bureaucracy and the power of questioning bears an analogy to the dilemmas of block. The officer found that there were once good reasons for standing there. And we have emphasized over and over that block, too, has its "good reasons," reflecting mechanisms that in general serve us well. The trouble is, when we're blocked we're responding to "good reasons" that have vanished or don't apply in this case. We're tangled in the usually efficient bureaucracy of the self. We're "holding the horses."

And the innovative officer who investigated the "why" is a model for us too. He stands for the power of inquiry, understanding and strategic action (for example, giving the two horse-

243

holders something better to do). So with block: when we can inquire into what's going on, come to understand the forces at work better, and make strategic use of the will, we are empowered.

Good thing, too. We all have agendas and aspirations. We all have visions of the best use to make of our time and our energies. We don't want to find ourselves "holding the horses" of traumas past or pressures present. With a modicum of intelligence, a good bit of strategizing, and a generous portion of persistence, we can often turn the horses loose—and ourselves as well. We *can* get out of our own way.

ENDNOTES

Chapter 1. COMMON SENSE FOR COMMON BLOCKS

Force: The Latent Metaphor
"The essence of metaphor . . .": Lakoff and Johnson (1980), p.5.
About the force/physics metaphor: Many formal psychological theories, as well as our everyday terms, reflect an underlying force metaphor. Freud's psychodynamic theory, in both name and nature, borrows a metaphoric system from the hydraulic paradigm of early 20th century physics. His theory includes the use of terms and concepts like energy, tension, impulse, power, driving and restraining forces, and repression. In the 1930s, Kurt Lewin's phenomenologically-oriented Social Field Theory found metaphoric inspiration in Einstein's theory of relativity. In Lewin's view, the individual occupies a psychological life space consisting of the person, the person's psychological environment (that is, how the person perceives the world), and the (non-psychological) world itself. Lewin talks about the relationships between all these factors as constituting a force field, which determines the individual's behavior. In the '40s and '50s, the study of human psychology was increasingly recognized as an appropriate focus for laboratory as well as clinical research and, in a way, psychology was no longer content to be *like* a physical science, it strove to *be* a physical science. Skinner's Behavior Theory, for example, explicitly focuses on describing cause-effect relationships between observable phenomena and considers human behavior only in physical and quantitative terms. All of these theorists in different ways model their understanding of human psychology on how objects behave in the physical world: i.e., they use

what we call here a "force" metaphor. Readers who would like to learn more about major psychological theorists, can begin by consulting a current introductory textbook on personality theory, such as Feschbach and Weiner (1986).

About metaphors and figurative language: Lakoff and Johnson (1980) have produced a very readable discussion of the variety of metaphors we use in our everyday language. Also, for a more formal discussion of the role of figurative language in the process of growth and healing, see Pollio, et al. (1977).

Everyday Force Theory
   "We strive in spite of ourselves . . .": Morimoto (1972).
   About the "reality" of psychological forces: Everyday Force Theory suggests that psychological forces are things we derive or infer, and even the idea of psychological forces is a human construction. But just because we "make up" these ways of describing the world as we experience it, that does not mean that the things we refer to are not "real." For instance, we have the terms "bushes" and "trees" to describe certain leafy parts of the world—but who is to say where the borderline between bushes and trees falls, or whether there are only two natural categories? Maybe someone from another culture or another planet has three terms; bushes, trees and trushes, with trushes tending somewhat larger than bushes and somewhat smaller than trees. Just because we make up convenient ways of talking, does not mean there *are* no trees or bushes. All these different sized leafy things are *really* there in the world. Likewise, it is a matter of our convenience and convention to identify specific factors that motivate our behavior, and even to make up a concept like psychological forces to refer collectively to these factors. For a fun and interesting discussion about the notion that reality is a human construction, see Watzlowick (1976, 1984). Even Freud (1920, p. 241), in discussing the nature of the unconscious, tipped his hat in recognition of this point when he wrote, "Our ability to give meaning to neurotic symptoms by means of analytic interpretation is an irrefutable indication of the existence of unconscious psychological process—or, if you prefer, an irrefutable proof of the necessity for their assumption." We will return to this matter of the "reality" of psychological forces in later chapters.

How Everyday Force Theory Explains . . .
Comic strip: *Rose is Rose* by Pat Brady, 8/18/86. Reprinted with the permission of United Feature Syndicate.

Chapter 2. BLOCKED IN, BLOCKED OUT

Epigraph
"When very bright people . . .": William G. Perry, Jr., is the founder of the Bureau of Study Counsel at Harvard University. He is well known as the creator of the "Perry Developmental Scheme" which describes how students' assumptions about the nature of knowledge change during their college years. See Perry (1970).

The Myth of Will Power
About free will and will power: Daniel C. Dennett, a professor of cognitive studies at Tufts University, explores the nature of the will in his book, *Elbow Room* (1984). He grapples with many of the same issues we explore here in our consideration of counterintentional behavior: issues of causality, control, self-definition, decision making and determinism, for example. Readers interested in exploring the psycho-philosophical territory of these issues will find his work intriguing. An essay by Raymond Smullyan, with commentary by Douglas Hofstadter (Smullyan, 1981), has a different take on the free-will issue. Smullyan chronicles a conversation between God and a Mortal, in which the Mortal beseeches God to absolve him of the horrible burden of free will, only to learn that free will is not a gift from God but a metaphysical *sine qua non* of human existence.
About Charles Whitman: Discussions of Whitman's case can be found in the neurological literature. There is some controversy as to whether Whitman's behavior was the direct result of his tumor. A brief summary of the case can be found in Sifakis (1982, p.761).

Sources of Forces
About the mind/body issue: In her recent book on the psychology of mindfulness and mindlessness, Ellen Langer includes a chapter on "Minding Matters: Mindfulness and Health." She describes research

which explores the relationship between mind and body, and discusses ways in which we can affect our health and well-being by developing our capacities for mindfulness (Langer, 1989).

A Circle of Causation

About the circle of causation: Theorists in many different fields have tried to describe the relationship between Organism and Environment. Some focus on the organism's effect on the environment, some focus on the environment's effect on the organism. Most recognize a continuous interplay between the two, something like the "circle of causation" presented here. A particularly interesting model of the feedback loop linking inner and outer reality can be found in Holland (1988). Holland is a literary critic who describes a cognitive approach to literature. See especially his Chapter 5, "We Are Round."

About psychotherapies and the circle of causation: Watzlowick et al., in *Change* (1974), vividly describe several clinical interventions that rely on reframing as a therapeutic technique. See especially their Chapter 9, "The Gentle Art of Reframing," pp. 92–110. For a more technical overview of several different cognitive-behavioral psychotherapeutic approaches which implicitly highlight different intervention points, readers should consult the special issue of *The Counseling Psychologist* (Fretz, 1988).

Chapter 3. MYSTERIOUSLY BLOCKED

Why Hidden Forces?

"When you have eliminated the impossible . . .": This comment was offered by the fictional sleuth, Sherlock Holmes, to his friend Dr. Watson. (Doyle, undated, page 54).

About hidden forces and the unconscious: The notion of hidden forces is clearly associated with the idea of the unconscious. For an extensive account of the history of this idea, readers should consult Ellenberger, *The Discovery of the Unconscious* (1970). Ellenberger suggests that the model of the human mind based on the duality of conscious and unconscious mechanisms is a surprisingly recent one, dating only from the 19th century. Long before hidden forces were associated with the modern notion of the unconscious, they were attributed to other factors. For example, people who behaved in nonintentional or ego-alienated ways were considered—and still are, in many traditions—to be possessed by gods or spirits.

Hidden forces, then, can either be attributed to factors like the unconscious that are recognized as *part of* the human integrity, or to factors like the Devil, which are seen as *invasions into* the human integrity. Furthermore, the line between these two understandings of hidden forces is often very fuzzy indeed, raising the question: How do we know who and what we are in the first place? An interesting and entertaining exploration of these issues can be found in Julian Jaynes' *The Origin of Consciousness* (1976).

Why Do Forces Get Hidden?
About forces being hidden by design: Sigmund Freud would probably have referred to the phenomena whereby forces get hidden by design as *defense mechanisms*. He suggests, for example, that the emergence of hysterical symptoms in response to trauma is the individual's defense against unbearable affect or unacceptable impulse. See his early work on the etiology of hysterical symptoms and his discussions of defense mechanisms in the *Complete Psychological Works*, Volumes I, II and VI.

Comic strip: *Sherman on the Mount* by Walt Lee, 11/21/86. Reprinted with the permission of the author.

Chapter 5: BLOCK UPON BLOCK

A Spiral of Causation
"We have nothing to fear . . .": Franklin Delano Roosevelt (1933).
About the self as both subject and object: The fields of ego development and object relations within psychology are both concerned with the process by which the boundaries of the Self are defined—how it is that some times we are "at one" with some aspects of our experience or the world, and at other times we have a more "objective" perspective

on it. In his wonderful book, *The Evolving Self* (1982), Robert Kegan describes a model of ego development across the lifespan that explores how the self is created and recreated, defined and transformed in recursive cycles of embeddedness and differentiation.

The Constructed Self

About the Self and Not-Self boundary: Our assumption that our skin forms the boundary between the Self and the Not-Self is a very basic one. We tend not to question it unless it is violated. For example, if a man told you he was not connected to his body—that he was outside his body—you would immediately think something was amiss. Most seriously you might wonder if he'd gone insane or ingested some sort of mind-altering substance. Or more benignly, you might think he had some sort of quirky belief in astral projection. The neurologist, Oliver Sacks (1985), documents a strange neurological impairment marked by an inability to recognize one's body, or a part of one's body, as one's own. He describes a patient who, waking up in a hospital bed, finds under the covers with him a gruesome detached leg. In disgust, the patient throws the leg out of the bed, only to land himself in a heap on the floor. The leg had been his own but he hadn't recognized it as his own.

Summary

"Every person . . .": Abraham Maslow (1965) p. 308.

Chapter 6. BLOCK LOCK

The Thrall of It All
"Isa Whitney . . .": Doyle (1975), p. 70.

Chapter 7. BLOCKS ON ALL SIDES

Blocked Between
About how one's answer depends on how the question is framed: See Tversky and Kahneman (1981).

Endnotes

Getting Out From Between

"Whenever you're called on . . .": Piet Hein (1966), p. 38. Reprinted by permission of MIT Press.

Self Sealing Situations

When an attempted solution perpetuates the problem: Leon Lipson (1964) coined the term "self-sealing." He recently related to us this illustration of a sealed system: In postwar Belgium, many young babies broke out in an unidentified rash. Mothers used liberal doses of baby powder to treat their unhappy infants and try to ease their discomfort, but the outbreak continued to worsen. It was finally determined that the rash was caused by . . . the baby powder!

The case of the over-helpful parents: Adapted from Watzlowick, Weakland and Fisch (1974), pp. 116–119.

Chapter 9. ANALYSIS, POETRY AND THE MIND'S REALITY

How Do You Size Up a Theory?

About the poetic side of other theories: We describe the poetry of force theory, but what of the poetry of other theories? Traditional psychodynamic theories, with their emphasis on the murky unconscious, their talk of unearthing suppressed thoughts or shoring up defenses against potential floodwaters of emotion or impulse, speak with what seems to us a powerful poetry of turbulent subterranean rivers. In contrast, Rogerian psychotherapy, with its emphasis on becoming oneself, on the uniqueness of each person and the importance of acceptance and reflection in therapy, offers what seems to us to be a rather calm and beautific poetry. Behaviorism, emphasizing stimulus-response patterns and behavioral conditioning, speaks in a rather cold and mechanical poetry.

Clearly we stereotype and oversimplify admittedly multi-faceted and profound theories to talk of their poetries in this way. You may not even agree with our assessment of these poetries; you may hear and feel something quite different in them than we do. In a way, that's the point. The poetic power of a theory lies in how well it reflects one's inner experience: two people with quite different inner experiences will react quite differently to a given theory's poetry.

About "truth" and "reality": The philosopher Alfred Schuetz talks about whether an objective "reality" exists. Schuetz points out that we each perceive the world from our own existentially unique vantage point, "the center O of my system of coordinates" (1945, p. 545), so no two of us perceive quite the same reality anyway. In addition, he notes that, "Strictly speaking, there are no such things as facts. All facts are from the outset facts selected from a universal context by the activities of our mind" (1953, p. 2). He concludes that reality is, literally, a matter of common sense—that is, a matter of consensual determination. Reality is what we all agree reality is.

BIBLIOGRAPHY

DENNETT, Daniel. *Elbow Room: The Varieties of Free Will Worth Wanting*. Cambridge: MIT Press, 1984.

DOYLE, Sir Arthur Conan. *The Sign of Four*. In *The Works of A. Conan Doyle*, New York: P.F. Collier and Son Company, Undated.

————, "The Man With the Twisted Lip." In *The Complete Adventures and Memoirs of Sherlock Holmes*, New York: Clarkson N. Potter, Inc., 1975.

ELLENBERGER, Henri F. *The Discovery of the Unconscious*. New York: Basic Books, 1970.

FESCHBACH, Seymour; WEINER, Bernard. *Personality*. 2nd edition, Lexington, MA: D.C. Heath & Co., 1986.

FRETZ, Bruce R. (ed.) "Special Issue: Cognitive-Behavioral Treatments of Anxiety." *The Counseling Psychologist*. Volume 16 (1), January 1988.

FREUD, Sigmund. *A General Introduction to Psychoanalysis*. Translated by G. Stanley Hall. New York: Boni & Liveright, 1920.

————. *The Complete Pschological Works of Sigmund Freud*. Standard Edition, edited by James Strachey, London: Hogarth Press, 1966.

HEIN, Piet. "A Psychological Tip." In *Grooks*. Cambridge, MA: The MIT Press, 1966.

HOFSTADTER, Douglas R. and DENNETT, Daniel C. *The Mind's I: Fantasies and Reflections on Self and Soul*. New York: Bantam Books, 1981.

HOLLAND, Norman N. *The Brain of Robert Frost*. New York: Routledge, 1988.

JAYNES, Julian. *The Origin of Consciousness in the Breakdown of the Bicameral Mind*. Boston: Houghton Mifflin, 1976.

KEGAN, Robert. *The Evolving Self: Problem and Process in Human Development*. Cambridge, MA: Harvard University Press, 1982.

LANGER, Ellen. *Mindfulness*. Reading, MA: Addison-Wesley Publishing Company, 1989.

LAKOFF, George and JOHNSON, Mark. *Metaphors We Live By*. Chicago: University of Chicago Press, 1980.

LIPSON, Leon. "How to Argue in Soviet." Unpublished lecture, Stanford University, April 1969.

MASLOW, Abraham. "Some Basic Propositions of a Growth and Self-Actualization Psychology." In G. Lindzey and C. Hall (eds.), *Theories of Personality: Primary Sources and Research*. New York: Wiley, 1965, pp. 307–316.

MORIMOTO, Kiyo, with the assistance of Judith Gregory and Penelope Butler. "On Trying to Understand the Frustrations of Students." (pamphlet), Bureau of Study Counsel, Harvard University, 1972.

PERRY, William G., Jr. *Forms of Intellectual and Ethical Development During the College Years*. New York: Holt, Rinehart and Winston, 1970.

POLLIO, Howard; BARLOW, Jack; FINE, Harlow; POLLIO, Marilyn. *Psychology and the Poetics of Growth: Figurative Language in Psychology, Psychotherapy, and Education*. Hillsdale NJ: Lawrence Erlbaum Associates, 1977.

ROOSEVELT, Franklin Delano. *First Inaugural Address*. 1933.

SACKS, Oliver. *The Man Who Mistook His Wife For a Hat*. New York: Summit Books, 1985.

SCHUETZ, Alfred. "On Multiple Realities." *Philosophy and Phenomenological Research*, v.V, June, 1945.

———— "Common Sense and Scientific Interpretation of Human Action." *Philosophy and Phenomenological Research*, v.XIV, September 1953.

SIFAKIS, Carl. *The Encyclopedia of American Crime*. New York: Facts on File, Inc., 1982.

Bibliography

SMULLYAN, Raymond M. "Is God a Taoist?" In Douglas R. Hofstadter and Daniel C. Dennett, *The Mind's I: Fantasies and Reflections on Self and Soul*. New York: Bantam Books, 1981, pp. 321–343.

TVERSKY, Amos; KAHNEMAN, Daniel. "The Framing of Decisions and the Psychology of Choice." Science, *211*, 1981, pp. 453–458.

WATZLOWICK, Paul; WEAKLAND, John; and FISCH, Richard. *CHANGE: Principles of Problem Formation and Problem Resolution*. New York: Norton, 1974.

WATZLOWICK, Paul. *How Real is Real?* New York: Random House, 1976.

WATZLOWICK, Paul. (ed.) *The Invented Reality*. New York: W.W. Norton & Company, 1984.